Bluffer's®
GUIDE TO
ENTERTAINING

BY WILLIAM HANSON

© Haynes Publishing 2019
First published August 2019

A CIP Catalogue record for this book
is available from the British Library.

ISBN: 978 1 78521 650 3 (print)
ISBN: 978 1 78521 684 8 (eBook)

Library of Congress control no. 2019942910

Published by Haynes Publishing,
Sparkford, Yeovil, Somerset BA22 7JJ
Tel: 01963 440635
Int. tel: +44 1963 440635
Website: www.haynes.com

Printed in Malaysia.

Series Editor: David Allsop.

CONTENTS

'The essence of the art of entertaining lies, I always think, in establishing an atmosphere of grace and decorum.'

Hyacinth Bucket

THAT'S ENTERTAINMENT

There are arguably few things in life which provide greater pleasure than welcoming guests into your home. Except, perhaps, to see them leave it – effusively thanking you for your hospitality.

Entertaining is an art. Like a musical instrument, it takes practice and tuning. Some hosts have a natural flair and can make it look effortless; others obsess for days just to prepare the simplest of kitchen suppers. It doesn't matter which category you fall into, as long as you get it right on the night. This can call for bluffing skills of the highest order, requiring you to pretend to each guest that the occasion would be diminished without their presence, however grindingly dull they might be. Some people do this for a living (God help them): it's called working in the 'hospitality industry' (or what used to be known as 'hotel and catering'). From the lowliest greasy spoon to the loftiest Michelin-starred restaurant, the rules are the same. The most important thing to remember about entertaining, as a professional or an amateur, and however irksome the realisation might be, is that your guests are the priority. If you are enjoying your own party too much then it probably means there is a guest somewhere looking for the lavatory, peering forlornly into an empty glass, or in need or rescuing from a tedious fellow guest.

Entertaining is not just about hosting a party: the most successful exponents of the art are just as good guests as they are hosts. It is true that there is generally a significantly smaller financial outlay when attending a bash, yet there should never be any economy on your wit, rapport and charm. Exemplary guests are few and far between and if you learn the social skills needed or – more aptly – bluff that you have the skills needed then you won't go far wrong.

If you are enjoying your own party too much, then it probably means there is a guest somewhere peering forlornly into an empty glass.

For those trying to bluff their way through successful entertaining, it is important to remember that confidence is the key. No guest will enjoy being hosted by someone who does not give the impression of relaxed and nonchalant self-belief in their ability to hold a good party. People have spent lifetimes trying to achieve this sense of effortless aplomb.

The bluffer hasn't got a lifetime to spare, so when you

next find yourself on the spot this short but definitive guide can offer invaluable help.

It sets out to conduct you through the main danger zones encountered in talking about entertaining – and then actually putting it into practice. It will also equip you with the vocabulary and evasive technique required to minimise the risk of being rumbled as a bluffer, and it will give you a few easy-to-learn hints and techniques that might even allow you to be accepted as a host of rare panache and experience. But it will do more.

It will give you the tools to impress legions of marvelling listeners with your knowledge and insight – without anyone discovering that, until you read this, you probably didn't know the difference between a masquerade and a maraschino cherry.

'A little party never killed nobody.'
(From the soundtrack to The Great Gatsby, *2013)*

LET'S HAVE A PARTY

Jay Gatsby, the fabulously wealthy 1920s fictional socialite and eponymous protagonist of the F. Scott Fitzgerald 'Jazz Age' novel, had a simple enough philosophy about how to hold a memorable party. Throw money at it, cast your invitations wide, and remain resolutely aloof from the proceedings. It doesn't sound like the sort of approach the average bluffer should adopt, and it's not one that this book would recommend – not least because nobody ever claimed that Gatsby was a particularly good host (just a very rich one). There is more to hosting than a lavish budget.

There are two essential rules omitted from the Gatsby code of entertainment, possibly because they are so blindingly obvious that they don't need to be stated. If you're holding a party, never run out of food or drink and don't ignore your guests. Failure to observe these simple pieces of advice will consign you to the scrap heap of eternally doomed hosts. By taking the right precautions (reading this book is a good start), you can make sure that you're not one of them.

This is more than just a practical and indispensable guide to how to pretend that you're a host of rare taste and distinction. It's also a guide to the dos and don'ts of entertaining guests. Many a host has set out with the best of intentions only to fall headlong into the elephant trap which the expert bluffer will have seen yawning from the other side of the party.

But before you decide you're going to do some entertaining, you should have in mind some idea of what sort of function it's going to be.

Newcomers to the challenging world of entertaining may be forgiven for finding the choice of different party types confusing, let alone the correct form to be observed at each, and might be surprised to learn that there is more involved than herding a group of people into a shared space and providing them with food and drink. There is much, much more to entertaining than that.

To begin, here's a brief guide to the various popular party options available to you. Even bluffers have to start somewhere.

BANQUETS

Very expensive to produce and not normally the done thing in a domestic setting. Indeed to call any occasion a 'banquet' is at worse pretentious, at best likely to raise expectations to unrealisable levels. So bluffers would be advised not to start with one. Banquets are the preserve of state visits, livery companies and City fat cat dinners. Banquets don't really work in a semi in the suburbs, not least because it's difficult to seat more than a dozen people in comfort and there's not much room for serving staff to manoeuvre around the table. But should you decide to hold one (or be tempted to call an ordinary dinner one) there should be numerous courses, one of which should not be a cheese plate. Cheese should never be served because it is historically considered peasants' food. And getting up to relieve yourself (call it 'going to the toilet' on pain of death*) during courses is perhaps one of the worst faux pas you could possibly make at such an occasion. So go easy on the drink.

Dress: white tie (sometimes black tie at lesser banquets). See page XX.

Length: 4+ hours (brace yourself).

BARBECUES

Anyone who considers a barbecue to be synonymous with good food is likely to be disappointed. At a barbecue everything looks and tastes the same and is either undercooked, overcooked and almost always badly cooked – usually all three at the same time. And there is usually rain. But now that the royal family has made the practice socially acceptable by holding regular summer barbecues at Balmoral, you might be tempted to host one yourself. The first rule about holding barbecues is: don't. The second, should you fail to heed the first, is don't try to compete with the royal family. It must be remembered that their barbecues include a proper table, linen napkins, tablecloths and knifes and forks

---

* *See The Bluffer's Guide to Etiquette*

that are not white, flimsy and plastic. The third rule is to have a professional prepare and cook the food in the kitchen, before going through the ceremony of turning the meat (which should really only be prime steak or gourmet burgers) into charcoal later in the garden. (At least you'll know it was once cooked properly.) And the fourth rule? Give your male guests a token barbecue set of their own. It helps them get in touch with their inner Neanderthal, where they can happily play with fire, grunt, and burn meat. But don't let them loose on anything other than sausages. And definitely don't let them cook any meat with a bone in it. It's far too complicated.

Dress: come as you are (best avoid gingham shirts or end up clashing with the tablecloth).

Length: 2–3 hours.

BRUNCH

This clumsy portmanteau word describes not quite a lunch, and not quite a breakfast. It is eaten around ten or eleven o'clock in the morning and is thought to be the invention of the British, although Americans would claim otherwise. On the other hand the latter lay claim to 'power breakfasts' as well (they can keep them) and the abomination known as 'the working lunch'. As any epicurean worth the name will tell you, lunch is to be savoured and not worked through.

If you should find yourself hosting a brunch, serve the food buffet-style (see below) or family style. Provide scrambled or poached eggs along with cooked meat in the form of bacon and sausages. And fish, along the lines of kedgeree or smoked salmon. Other sundries might include pastries, and some indigestible lumps of flour, baking powder and dried fruit known as 'muffins'. And don't forget Champagne or the ubiquitous Prosecco – after all it is nearly lunch.

Dress: smart casual.

Length: 2–3 hours.

BUFFETS

Buffets range from the sumptuous to the sadly underwhelming. A table or two of platters of hopefully well-presented and appetising looking food is offered and guests help themselves. Most people are familiar with the concept, and thus might also be familiar with that moment when they reach the front of the queue to discover that the food has run out. So the first thing bluffers should do is to make sure there is enough to go round. There is nothing more guaranteed to undermine your reputation as a host than the food running out while half the guests are patiently queuing with empty plates. Again, employ professionals and give them accurate numbers.

Dress: smart casual.

Length: until the food disappears.

CHEESE & WINE PARTIES

Terribly 1960s, but rather fun in a post-ironic sort of way. There is only one rule when it comes to pairing cheeses with wine: there should never be any pineapple on a cocktail stick. The idea is that wedges of different varieties of cheese are grouped by country, colour, animal and type while copious amounts of wine, sometimes of doubtful provenance, are poured from bottles rather than decanters so that guests can supposedly make appreciative noises while reading the labels. There is, actually, one other rule: never cut the 'nose' off a wedge of cheese – it's generally the ripest, and most prized, part of the cheese round – and therefore not good manners. Cheeses should be cut in thin lengths from the rind to the centre. As a host, you should ensure that all cheeses are flagged, indicating what they are and where they're from, and make absolutely sure that each cheese has its own knife (to prevent flavour contamination).

Dress: smart casual.

Length: 2 hours.

CHRISTENING PARTIES

These take place after an infant's baptism, often in the parental home or sometimes in a 'function room' of a church, although if this option is going to be taken, opt for the cloisters (far smarter). Fruitcake is often served – frequently it is the top tier of the parents' wedding cake. Should the parents not yet have got married, perish the thought, the top tier of the Christening party cake might be saved for the wedding cake. It's a topsy-turvy old world.

Dress: lounge suits.

Length: 2 hours.

COFFEE MORNINGS

These are a well-established means of providing a relaxed, informal networking environment for local business people and anyone with a commercial interest within relevant communities. But they're not just about business, having begun as a popular rendezvous for 'yummy mummies', local worthies, church volunteers, and anybody with a charitable drum to beat. As host, you are permitted to charge for each cup of coffee (it should always be freshly made, never instant, and don't forget decaf and tea) ensuring that the proceeds go to the nominated charity. The 'entertainment' can be something like a tombola, and/or a raffle. Less-than-inspiring prizes often get recycled with the items only disappearing once they reach their sell-by date. Try to be a little more imaginative with these (ask the local pub to donate a complimentary dinner for two, and the golf and tennis clubs a free lesson.) Bring along at least £20 in pound coins (some in 50-pence pieces) to ensure that you can provide change for the person who 'only has a tenner'.

Dress: smart casual (twinsets, pearls and business suits permitted).

Length: 2 hours.

DINNER PARTIES

These have got rather a bad name since the advent of the painfully addictive TV series *Come Dine With Me* (which you must never admit to watching). Before then, they were unrivalled as the most effective and enjoyable of all forms of entertaining. Hence they are considered more extensively in a later chapter.

Dress: nowadays often smart casual.

Length: 3–4 hours (weekday ones will be shorter than weekend ones).

HEN PARTIES

Organised by women for their friends, frequently – but not always – in advance of a wedding. In modern Britain these usually take the form of drunken nights out on a pub crawl. There is no useful part that a bluffer can play at a hen party, unless you're a man and you arrive as a male stripper. But this is not advised if you value your dignity and are easily humiliated.

Dress: pink cowboy hats, very short skirts.

Length: if you're not drunk it'll feel much longer than it actually is.

DRINKS & COCKTAIL PARTIES

Bluffers should know that the basic difference between these two very similar occasions is that cocktails are served at a cocktail party, and wine, Champagne and beer are served at a drinks party. A cocktail is generally something that has three or more ingredients. It's important that you get this right. It's not difficult. They too are considered in more detail in another chapter.

Dress: smart casual.

Length: 2–3 hours.

GARDEN PARTIES

You really need an expansive and impressive lawn in order to properly host a decent garden party. If you don't have one, they're not too hard to find. Most country hotels have them, but if you really want to win your spurs as someone who knows their entertaining onions, hire a National Trust property. Or combine the two. Cliveden, in Berkshire, is a former stately home and now one of the country's great luxury hotels. More importantly, it's got nearly 400 acres of National Trust managed formal gardens and parkland. You won't need that many, but it's nice to have the option. And, just as importantly, you get a scandal thrown in for free (the house and its gardens featured prominently in the Profumo affair).

Dress: smart casual unless otherwise stated (and beware high heels getting stuck in the lawn).

Length: 2–3 hours.

HOUSEWARMINGS

These are usually drinks receptions but with a reason (to 'warm' the new house). The grander the house, the grander the party. Housewarmings originate from the days before central heating – it was customary for each guest to bring firewood (as the hostess gift) making fires in every fireplace in the house. However unlikely this sounds it is, in fact, true. There is no need to expect your guests to bring a log or two these days. A bottle of something warming, or a gift voucher for a furniture shop or department store is usually more welcome – as long as neither is mistaken for fuel. Try not to show too much disdain if a Scottish guest arrives with a frog. These are supposed to represent good luck, but not necessarily for the frog or the hostess.

Dress: smart casual.
Length: 2–3 hours.

KITCHEN SUPPERS

Casual gatherings around a rustic kitchen table, where the guests often watch the host cook. This is only recommended if the host *can* cook and guests can be reasonably confident that whatever is being served up will be relatively digestible. Sensible bluffers will serve up something they prepared much earlier – such as a hotpot, casserole or stroganoff. Don't be too ambitious, and don't feel that you need to provide a first course. A good nourishing main course, followed by a simple pudding and/or a good cheese plate is all that is expected of you.

Dress: come as you are.
Length: 2 hours.

MURDER MYSTERY NIGHTS

Terrible, awkward evenings where the host thinks everyone will have a great time dressing up in 1970s garb and finding their inner-actor. In reality, most guests are hoping an actual murder will take place instead. Incredibly stressful to organise, on top of dinner and drinks, and rarely appreciated.

Dress: varies on theme (don't bother spending too much).
Length: forever.

PICNICS

There is nothing so peculiarly British as a picnic in the pouring rain. How many other nations' citizens willingly huddle under a tree in a thunderstorm munching on sticks of limp celery and waiting for the skies to clear? The British enthusiasm for a picnic is unquestionably the triumph of hope over experience, because they never quite live up to expectations. Even if you get a sunny day, instead of the distant drone of honey bees in the hazy

---

'Picnics are for ants' (Anon)

---

distance, you're more likely to be fending off swarms of wasps, aggressive gulls and myriad crawling insects. Enjoy! And don't forget the corkscrew. The first lesson the picnic bluffer must learn is to organise them spontaneously, waiting for one of those rare moments when the sky is cloudless. Find somewhere relatively peaceful with a view, and always remember to clear up YOUR rubbish. Your guests will be watching.

Dress: casual.
Length: 2–3 hours.

POTLUCK SUPPER

Each guest brings a dish to be enjoyed by the group, often in a buffet format. While it might be assumed that these types of gatherings require little preparation or effort, there will always be one person who has skilfully organised who is bringing what and assigned the worst cook the task of bringing the salad, or – if their culinary 'achievements' are notorious – the drink. That person doing the delegating will be you, because you will nominally be the host and providing the venue.

Dress: smart casual.

Length: 3–4 hours depending on how many courses.

SAFARI SUPPER

These are to be found in the suburban jungle where the guests can walk to a different house in the same street or neighbourhood for a different course. One person hosts the pre-dinner drinks, the next house the first course, and so on and so forth. You, as the organiser, will be providing the most challenging part of the entertainment – the main course. Remember: this is not a competition. (Well, actually it is.)

Dress: smart casual.

Length: 4–5 hours (the walking makes it longer).

STAG PARTIES

A congregation of increasingly drunken men behaving badly usually held in advance of a wedding. Assuming that you're charged with the responsibility of arranging one of these and providing the entertainment, bear in mind that your most important role is to keep the groom alive and out of harm's way. That's it really, and you'll just have to get used to the frequently levelled accusation that you're a boring killjoy. It's a thankless task, and one which you should delegate and avoid if at all possible.

Dress: anything you don't care about, on the grounds that you'll probably never see it again.

Length: interminable; sometimes they go on for whole weekends, and longer.

WEDDING BREAKFASTS

Today they are mainly referred to as 'receptions', but correctly they are known as wedding breakfasts. Weddings are no place for the bluffer to venture. Serious professionals will be at work here, and if you dare to pretend to be an expert in organising a wedding (with no previous experience) you'll be exposed faster than you could ever have imagined possible.

Dress: lounge suits or morning dress.

Length: 9 hours if you're lucky, 6 if you're not.

ß

'You got the invitation
You got the right address
You need some medication?
The answer's always yes.'
(From the soundtrack of the 2016 film La La Land*)*

BE MY GUEST

Entertaining should look almost effortless, and to achieve that you need ... effort, even if it is largely alien to the bluffer's creed.

Parties don't just happen organically, expert hosts apply often military-style planning with forensic attention to detail. And, therefore, so must you – or at least pretend to. With practice, they become easier – experienced hosts will sometimes find a menu and routine that works, and then repeat it unapologetically, only changing the guests each time. No one need know that you cooked the same combination of food, paired with the same wine, accompanied by the same table decorations only very recently. Ambitious hosts will even attempt a drinks party and a dinner party on consecutive nights – saving the cost of fresh floral decorations and the need to carry out extensive cleaning (make sure that you have the drinks party on the second night, because the mess will be significantly worse). Bluffers will be well advised to think carefully before inflicting this sort of punishing challenge on themselves.

It is probably best saved for much later in their hospitality careers.

THE GUEST LIST

Once you have decided upon the type of entertainment you want to put on, the next step is to draw up the guest list. For a dinner party the numbers will be limited to the number of people you can (comfortably) fit around the dining table. Be realistic, and don't expect your guests to squeeze into a shoulder width space on the corner of the table. And bear in mind that not too many people will appreciate having a table leg between their own. In more elevated dining circles 21 inches of space is the minimum width expected for each place setting (although 30 inches is generally considered to be the ideal size). And it is often forgotten how much space should be allowed behind each diner's seat. The answer is 24 inches when someone is sitting in it. Finally, make sure that your table doesn't have too low an apron – the panel beneath the table top. There should be enough space between knees and table undersides for guests to cross their legs in comfort.

The size of the guest list for a drinks party or buffet depends on the size of your reception rooms or chosen venue, and only you can be the judge. Again, avoid at all costs making guests feel like they are playing the parlour game 'sardines' (unless, of course, they *are* playing the parlour game of 'sardines').

Don't make the mistake of trying to find a date which suits everyone on your preferred guest list. This will never work satisfactorily, so don't give your invitees a choice. The only exception to this is to check with a shortlist of preferred guests if they can make the date you have in mind, but be discreet how you ask them, as in a casual: 'I was thinking of holding a light supper/cocktail/Hallowe'en party and wondered if you might be able to drop by on Saturday the XXth.' The best advice, as in most things, is to plan ahead. Don't expect too many people to be free at a few days' notice, other than those people who don't have a previous engagement (for which there might be a very good reason).

Nobody ever blames the host when trouble kicks off between guests (but try to conceal your delight when it does).

There are websites such as Doodle.com, a scheduling tool that allows prospective attendees at any sort of gathering to look at a range of dates and find which work best (it used to be known as a diary) but this rather takes the shine out of the event before it's even begun. As above secure the attendance of your key guests and then if other guests invited can't come: tough. You have still at least asked them and added to your social capital by doing so. There is no place for democracy in party planning.

Balance is key at any event – you might wish to steer clear of inviting two or more guests who are known to be vocal in their opinions about everything, especially if you know they are at polar opposites of the political spectrum. Politics and dinner parties don't mix (actually politics and anything don't mix) and even seating your pompous polemicists at opposite ends of a twelve-seater table will not stop them from putting a perfectly pleasant dinner at risk.

Of course, a guest list can be used mischievously for your own entertainment if you are of a certain kind of Machiavellian bent. Putting sworn enemies together, or former lovers, or a Remoaner next to a Brextremist, or other people who you suspect won't get on can be rather rewarding if you enjoy experimenting with group dynamics. Sometimes, inevitably, you will be confounded by people you had expected to gouge lumps out of each other getting on like a house on fire and becoming firm friends. But that's one of the joys of dinner parties – they can be full of surprises. And you can claim the credit when they're pleasant surprises. Conversely, nobody ever blames the host when trouble kicks off between guests (but it's always a good idea to conceal your delight when it does).

Similarly, if you're the matchmaking type, a dinner party is as good a milieu as any to put two singles together who you think would make an ideal match. Seat them near each other but do not interfere or let the other guests know what you're up to – someone is bound to make an ill-timed joke or remark that gives the game away. If anything is going to happen, it will happen naturally.

It is not generally acceptable for guests to ask hosts who else is going before they accept their own invitation, unless they are close friends – although this is the first question millennial guests will ask. Hosts who get posed this question by less well known invitees should simply reply, 'I'm still confirming names – but I'd love it if you can make it.' Then place an asterisk by their name as possible last minute cancellers, and thus future black listers.

An A list and a B list is often drawn up, with those at the top of the B list only invited if/when A-listers can't attend. Those planning weddings often use this tactic. Never admit to it.

For larger events, an A list and a B list is often drawn up, with those at the top of the B list only invited if/when A-listers can't attend. Those planning weddings often use this tactic. Never admit to it. And certainly don't confide to anybody that they should count themselves lucky that they've been upgraded to the A list. This particular practice underlines how important it is that invitations are accepted or declined promptly. If somebody receives an invitation to a wedding less than two months before the date, they can be reasonably sure that they were on a long list and that somebody has cancelled or declined, especially if they know that mutual friends received an invitation sometime before them. Weddings are planned so far in advance that it is inconceivable that invitations would be sent out just two months beforehand. In such circumstances many invitees choose to play a similar game and delay replying until the last possible moment. This sends a message to the host that they know they're B-listers (known as 'blisters' in the wedding planning game) and they're not impressed. It can get very messy. No wonder weddings are so stressful.

INVITATIONS (NEVER 'INVITES')

Once the guest list has been decided, the invitations can be issued. Increasingly this is done by telephone, email, or social networks. The guests, or their diary secretaries, will be telephoned to check availability and, if they can attend, a proper, formal invitation is posted a few weeks before the event. The expense involved in printing and sending invitations in the traditional way means that the practice is now virtually absent from everyday entertaining, sadly, but you can still judge the tone of the impending party by the invitation. If it comes via Facebook, you're probably not going to be expected to dress up. Whereas a stiffie through your letterbox heralds something all together more formal.

The most common example of the stiffie (no lewdness intended) is the wedding invitation. It must always be printed; anything else would devalue the occasion and suggest that costs are being cut (which doesn't presage a particularly lavishly hosted event). For all formal invitations, which generally suggest that the occasion is a special one and that it is a privilege to be invited, there are general rules of thumb as to what goes where – as follows.

The guest's name is written, by hand in blue or black ink in the top left. In the centre is the main information (who, where, when). In the bottom left are the RSVP details (if an address is listed, you write your reply, if a telephone number is listed, you may call, if a Twitter handle is listed think twice about attending). The bottom right has the additional information (what, when, dress code etc.).

Male hosts are not 'at Home' they simply 'request the pleasure of your company'. Ladies have 'at Home' printed as the second line instead. Stock 4 x 6 inch cards are easily acquired from all good stationers with the name of the host, the at home/request the pleasure line, and the RSVP details pre-printed onto the 4 x 6 inch card (ideally cream or ivory in colour but white is now fine, too). Everything else is written by hand by the host. This saves printing bespoke invitations for each event – although special occasions, such as a landmark birthday or anniversary do warrant the expense of exclusive invitations.

For funerals invitations of any kind do not get sent. Always remember: you don't get a stiffie for a stiffie.

MUSICAL CHAIRS

Even for a casual kitchen supper, having some semblance of a seating plan will help. Guests like to be placed and it is quite easy to avoid any awkward hovering around the table by being demonstrative and presenting the seating plan with no room for negotiation. Use name cards if you want.

In formal dining, the male guest of honour goes to the right of the hostess, the second male guest of honour to her left. The female guest of honour is seated to the right of the host, the second female guest of honour to his left.

As for exactly where on the table these key players sit depends on whether English- or French-style seating has been deployed. Yes, there are differences between the two nations. Who would have thought it? Bluffing hosts must know the difference.

If there are to be thirteen round the table then you have the perfect opportunity to bluff about your knowledge of 'Triskaidekaphobia', an irrational fear of the number 13.

With French-style seating, the key players sit along the table on the wider lengths. In English seating the hosts sit at the narrow ends of the table, with the guest of honour to their right. Just to confuse everybody, for state banquets at Windsor Castle the British royal family is said to prefer the French style of seating. When at Buckingham Palace they use three, long rectangular tables arranged in a U – a practice that dates back to the court of Henry VIII.

At informal dining occasions it is unlikely that

there will be any guests of honour, in which case you could seat the oldest female guest to the host's right, and so on. This is up to you, but it runs the risk of one or both female guests seething about presumptions made about their age. So probably best to ignore it. But whatever seating place you have in mind, try to not seat married couples (or couples that have been together for some time) next to each other. Boy–girl–boy–girl is usually the best policy, never husband–wife–boyfriend–girlfriend.

If there are to be thirteen round the table then you have the perfect opportunity to bluff about your knowledge of 'Triskaidekaphobia', an irrational fear of the number 13, long entrenched in the Christian tradition. You can start by blaming Judas Iscariot, the last apostle to take his place at the Last Supper bringing the number present up to 13. Then allude to an institution called the Thirteen Club in late 19th century New York which had as one of the central tenets of its charter a professed intention to rid the world of superstition. At its first meeting 13 dinner guests walked through the door, under a ladder, and sat between small mounds of spilt salt. Over the next half-century the club membership reportedly grew to include five future US presidents including Teddy Roosevelt.

As a good host you might also entertain the idea of every man moving three places to their right after each course. This is a great idea in theory (especially if your initial *placement* hasn't worked) but if things are going well, why take the risk of ruining a good party? Judge the atmosphere and guests before imposing a rotation.

FOOD, GLORIOUS, FOOD

As with the mix of guests, think about balance when it comes to your own choice of food. Some key points to consider before devising any menu are …

- **Time of year**. For winter opt for heavier, more substantial dishes; summer, lighter, more delicate offerings.
- **Can I actually cook this?** There is no point trying to attempt lobster foam and seared cockles in a seaweed jus if you have never done it before and are not known for your cooking skills. Don't be tempted to take on an unnecessary culinary challenge. Just offer something simple and tasty rather than trying to impress with something too adventurous.
- **Can I prepare 80% of this in advance?** As a host you want to spend most of the time with your guests rather than slaving away in the kitchen, sweating over the swordfish. Try to have only one course out of the three or four that requires a decent chunk of your attention on the night.
- **Will it go with the other courses?** You can disguise the fact it's your first time hosting by avoiding the trap that so many novice hosts fall into – think about how each dish complements each other. For example, don't serve soup as a first course (which is 'slow-release' food that will slowly make your guests feel fuller as they tuck into future courses), followed by a big bit of beef Wellington, followed by chocolate fondant. Far too rich and filling. Balance light and shade!

- **Source and use only seasonal local produce.**
  Claiming that this is central to your ethos as a host
  is the best bluff you can pull off. Who knows – it
  might become a habit. Spread the word – 'Eat with
  the seasons; it's cool'. Never, for example, serve
  asparagus in February (the season is late May to late
  July). And never serve anything where the dreaded
  spectre of food miles might hover in the wings, like
  Banquo's ghost at the feast.

SAY CHEESE

Cheese in Britain is generally served after the pudding
(in France it often comes before the sweet course and
in some American homes they serve cheese right at
the start, with the aperitifs: something of a novelty).
When the cheeseboard is presented it should be set
in a logical order with the mildest cheese on one side,
working across the board (left to right) to the strongest.
You can't force your guests to eat cheese this way but if
they know their Asiago from their Emmental then they
should know the form.

You can complement the board with quince paste,
sticks of celery and various chutneys if you wish. If
serving grapes, avoid grape scissors on pain of social
suicide.

CHEESEBOARD TIPS …
- Provide one knife per cheese.
- Serve with crackers or baguette (the French serve
  bread, the English biscuits – preferably high-baked

water biscuits, digestives, or cream crackers. You can introduce Ritz Crackers in a post-ironic way).

- Don't forget salted butter. It's a peculiarly British thing to have butter with your cheese.
- If possible identify the cheeses with little labels or flags for the uninitiated.
- While the purists will flinch, having a dairy-free cheese on standby for the lactose intolerant is a good idea and considerate – present this on a separate plate to avoid confusion or potential hospital runs.

BLUFFING BUFFETS

Place the buffet table in a logical place in a room. Look at the space available and imagine a queue of your guests – do they have space to queue? Is it clear where they start and end? A buffet table should have a flow, and guests should begin at one end and move towards the other, without having to go back to the start. The start should be where the plates are. No surprise there then, unless you expect them to wander about with a handful of Coronation Chicken. Cutlery and napkins (in lesser joints this is cutlery rolled into a napkin) should be at the other end. You will be easily spotted as a buffet bluffer if you place cutlery and napkins the same end as the plates; this will make your guests have to grapple with plate and cutlery as they serve themselves the food. Far more sensible for them to pick up their eating utensils once they have served themselves.

Make sure platters are replaced before they get to two-thirds empty – no one is going to take a sad and lonely looking piece of beef, but remove the platter to the kitchen, add some more beef round the lone slice and replace. And what d'you know? Someone's eaten it.

MUSIC

Music at larger parties is generally advisable. It can create an ambience and disguise the fact that there is some self-conscious chatter from the first guests to arrive. At smaller gatherings it can often be intrusive and annoying. If the desired balance of characters has been achieved then you needn't worry about supplementing it.

Karaoke (the Japanese word for 'bloody awful racket') is best avoided.

You will, naturally, be judged on your musical choice. Do you go live or digital? Live is best reserved for larger parties where there is space for a band, jazz group or even a harpist if you want to strike a celestial note (best avoided at funeral wakes). Digital music through some quality speakers is acceptable for more intimate affairs, but choose your selection well. Heavy metal and thrash probably isn't the best choice for a diamond anniversary. And having the radio playing is never a good idea – adverts for motor insurance and payday loans as you serve the fish course are unlikely to add to the ambience.

Old favourites with lyrics can distract guests into singing along rather than taking part in the conversation, and similarly songs that everyone loves (even instrumental versions) can distract too much. Whatever you opt for should be subtle and kept in the background.

Karaoke (the Japanese word for 'bloody awful racket') is best avoided. The Chinese and Japanese love it for reasons that defy explanation. It's best to leave them to it.

CHEATING WITH CATERING

No one is expecting you to do everything and serve everyone – especially if the guest list exceeds 60. You needn't try to be Martha Stewart. Indeed, the infamous American domestic doyenne started out by running a company that arrived the day before a party, took away all the hostess's serving dishes, pots & pans, then arrived the next day with all the food in said saucepans and tureens, together with a page of final instructions for warming up and finishing off so hostesses could pretend they had slaved away over a hot stove for days. It was a brilliant business model, and impossible to resist (if you could afford it).

Although that method may seem somewhat dishonest, getting in staff to help you cook, clean, serve (or all three) today is not unheard of and certainly shouldn't be considered taboo. Perhaps you should just be bold and admit to it. After all, it's just another way of using caterers.

VENTURING OUTSIDE

As delightful as the thought of an outdoors party is, Britain doesn't really have the weather for it – even in the summer months. The evening may start off promisingly but by sunset it starts to get a bit nippy and your guests begin to do that thing where they pretend they aren't cold, but the women are surreptitiously pulling on their partners' jackets. For those who wish to stay outside, then make sure there are some strategically placed terrace heaters (never *patio* heaters), that there is a terrace, and that there is some shelter. Thoughtful hosts will also have a supply of bug-repellent to hand. You can't be too careful.

'Be not forgetful to entertain strangers, for by this some have entertained angels without knowing it.'

(Hebrews 12:3)

HOSTS WITH THE MOST

ON THE DOORSTEP

Where do your guests put their coats when they arrive? It's the first thing they'll think of as they step over the threshold, followed closely by where to find a drink and details of your WiFi password. This is why most 'party experts' always recommend that before the guests arrive, you should pretend to be one of them and do a dry run. If you're not an experienced host, but you're bluffing that you are, you need to cover all the bases.

Ask yourself what they'll ask. How do they find you? How far are you from a station? If they come by car where do they park? If you're in town, where do they leave the car where they won't come back to find it on bricks, or gone, or being hoisted on to a tow-away truck?

If you're in the country, put some clearly visible signs out, and don't direct them to a soggy field full of manure or spitting llamas. How will your female guests' footwear cope? It might be a good idea to provide signs to a drop-off point near the front door. Mud-caked stilettos are never a good look and can lead to being mistaken for a parking warden spiking litter, covered in llama spit.

Approach the venue, wherever it is. Walk up the drive, or the steps, or off the street. Is the number/name of the house easily identifiable? Will anyone be at the door to greet guests? Will the bell be heard? Will guests feel comfortable pushing at an open door? Will they be asked who they are by someone they don't know? Nobody ever feels completely at ease entering a strange environment until they recognise a familiar face. Ideally there will be a hallway, or reception area, and if so the host should hover around it until all the expected guests are accounted for. Never offer drinks at the arrival point – your guests will stay to chat and never move on. Greet, shake, kiss (if appropriate) and then offer to remove coats – which should be assisted by any staff you might have hired for the event.

Do say May I help remove your coat?
Don't say May I take your coat?

It's a semantic nuance but a certain type of pedant will be impressed, and you will avoid the Inspector Clouseau moment in *The Return of the Pink Panther* where an opportunistic thief asks that latter question of Clouseau in a hotel lobby before walking off with his mac.

If your coat stand or rack near the entry point is inadequate for the number of guests, then employ any spare space and use a self-assembly coat rack (surprisingly inexpensive, but then they aren't things of beauty). Don't use a bed; people can never find where they left what, and it always ends up in the sort of heap Tracey Emin would be proud of.

BOTTOMS UP

Firmly point arriving guests at any room large enough to contain them, preferably not the same room where they'll be eating, and ensure that drinks are available either on a prominently sited table near the door or, preferably, on a tray held by a radiantly smiling member of staff. Welcome drinks will include a choice of red, white, or sparkling wine, mineral water and orange juice. You can of course demonstrate your man/woman of the people credentials by including a bucket containing bottles of iced beer as an option. Your staff will have been instructed to ask, 'In a glass, or by the neck Sir/Madam?' Smarter guests will always ask for beer in a glass. Only infants drink from bottles.

RECEIVING LINES

A receiving line of the hosts and guests of honour (if any) is really only for events such as weddings, key anniversaries or significant birthday parties where the guest list exceeds 100. If you decide to have one, ensure that it is not lined up until most guests are accounted for, and it's almost time to sit down to eat. Otherwise you might find yourself standing and thumb-twiddling as the stragglers drift in.

If the host's partner or guest of honour's partner is

female then it is the done thing to have 'an extra man' on the end, as it is strictly not done in social settings to end a receiving line with a woman.

Guests must be encouraged to exchange only the briefest of words with those in the line-up in order to keep things moving. Most will forget this, and a gentle nudge along the lines of 'I'm going to have to chivvy you Uncle Len, I can see people growing beards at the back of the queue – and that's just the ladies. ...'

INTRODUCTIONS

As host, one of your many duties is to ensure that everyone has someone to talk to. Most people will know the very basic etiquette that one should give a piece of information, ideally a common link, between the two people you are introducing. More advanced hosts, and this is what you strive to be, will know that there is a correct way to make such introductions.

Men and women are introduced, women first: 'Tallulah Marchbanks, may I introduce Gregory Gartside?'

Juniors and seniors are introduced, seniors first: 'Granny, may I introduce Annie?'

Lower and senior ranks are introduced seniors first: 'Mr President, may I introduce Nigel Dearlove from the Grimsby branch?'

And then the area of common ground is provided, followed by your exit line: 'Tallulah has just returned from a year in Mumbai, and I believe your father used to be stationed there, Gregory? Oh dear, I've just spotted Uncle

Len trying to find the lavatory. Tallulah, Gregory, would you excuse me and I'll catch up with you both later.'

Bluffers will know that while deliberate repetition of names is helpful to effect a memorable introduction, the practice of repeating the introduction in reverse ('June this is Henry, Henry this is June') should never be adopted. This will show your regrettable inexperience in these matters.

One of the most effective techniques in entertaining is to keep on the move, 'working' a room, keeping an eye out for people standing alone, rounding them up and steering them to a nearby group, introducing them, and then moving on again. It's hard work, but who said entertaining was easy? Here's a tip: always carry a bottle of fizz with you, top up glasses where necessary, and avoid getting bogged down by gesturing to the bottle and saying 'Sorry, duty calls!'

THE SURPRISE VEGAN

It is the guests' responsibility upon accepting your kind invitation to any party with a sit-down meal (NB: invitations should always invariably be preceded by the adjective 'kind') to alert their hosts as to any dietary requirements. Experienced hosts may wish to check with any new guests that they don't have any life-threatening allergies and so pre-empt the impending drama of them dropping like a stone when they get a whiff of peanut in an exotic Nasi Goreng starter. What's worse, and frankly very poor form, is a guest who suddenly reveals they are vegan, rendering your Osso Bucco useless.

Wise hosts will have learned lessons in the past from catering for the surprise vegan and so will always be stocked with something suitable to serve up. But it is not just vegans that you need worry about, even the vegetarians come in different shapes and sizes.

	Do serve	Don't serve
Ovo-vegetarians	Vegetables, fruit, nuts, eggs and honey	Poultry, meat, fish or dairy
Lacto-vegetarians	Vegetables, fruit, nuts, dairy (milk, gelatin-free yoghurt, butter, rennet-free cheese) and honey	Poultry, meat, fish or eggs
Lacto-ovo-vegetarians *(the most common type of vegetarian)*	Vegetables, fruit, nuts, eggs, dairy (milk, gelatin-free yoghurt, butter, rennet-free cheese) and honey	Poultry, meat or fish
Vegans	Vegetables, fruit, nuts, soups (made with soya cream)	Eggs, dairy products, honey, meat, poultry
Pescatarians	Fish, seafood, vegetables, nuts, dairy (milk, gelatin-free yoghurt, butter, rennet-free cheese) and honey	Poultry or meat
Pollotarians	Poultry, vegetables, dairy (milk, gelatin-free yoghurt, butter, rennet-free cheese) and honey	Meat or fish

Once in a blue moon you get a guest who is gluten intolerant, vegan, allergic to nuts, oh, of course, allergic to eggs and, just for good measure, is lactose intolerant. This is what experienced hosts refer to as DEFCON1. There is an easy solution that will help save time and effort when you suspect you might have a fussy eater coming – just ask them what they *can* eat – or, better still, get them to bring their own food. If they're still not sure, you might paraphrase Woody Allen in the film *Annie Hall* and suggest: 'Maybe some alfalfa sprouts and a plate of mashed yeast?'

PROBLEM DRINKERS

If you're confronted with a drunken guest you should stop serving them alcohol immediately. Get someone to call a cab, and hopefully the guest will be drunk enough to think they might have ordered it, and depart without causing a scene. This is where apps like Uber are very helpful as you can enter the destination on your phone and can check on the journey to see if the guest has arrived home safely.

If a confrontation develops with other guests, your primary role is to step in, stop it, and try not to get punched.

If all else fails, whisper into the drunk's ear: 'I've got a very special Single Malt next door. Come and have a dram.' When they're safely seated pour a generous measure of Scotch Bonnet chilli sauce into a glass, saying that the best way to savour it is 'down-in-one'. Nothing is better guaranteed to sober up a drunk, remarkably quickly. They'll feel like they've swallowed the sun.

TOASTS & SPEECHES

A toast is not a speech. The toast proposer should start by standing up, and his main function is getting the rest of the assembled guests standing. Tapping the glass with a knife is simply not done, but a repeated (and increasingly tetchy) 'Ladies and Gentlemen, may I have your attention please', is perfectly acceptable (and usually expected).

Once everyone is standing, the proposer raises his glass, proposes his toast and sits down. End of toast. Start of speeches.

Never toast with an empty glass – it is considered bad luck. Rules about not toasting with anything other than alcohol are nonsense. Water is fine.

Speeches after dinner should have the merit of brevity. As the old adage has it: a speech should be like a girl's skirt – long enough to cover the vital parts, but short enough to be interesting.

GUEST EXPECTATIONS

To be a gracious guest is an art – just as important as being an hospitable host. If you play the game correctly and come to any function armed with amusing anecdotes, charming manners and a good hostess gift you can ensure you will be much in demand and invited again. Look no further than Noël Coward – the master wit and raconteur – who rose from very humble origins to become the most sought after society guest in the English-speaking world. The irony is that he wasn't exactly known for his hosting skills. But he was a peerless entertainer. Every party needs one.

RSVP-ING

Take as much care when you reply to an invitation, as you might expect potential guests to take when replying to yours. Most people, with even the most limited knowledge of French, know what RSVP stands for – but many pronounce the S in the first word … except that it doesn't actually exist. Bluffers should know that it is *'répondez s'il vous plaît'* not *'réspondez'*.

Whatever form the invitation takes, electronically or by hand, it is fundamental that it gets replied to within a few days. Three to four days is really the limit. As a host you will make a mental note about those who slip up in this respect. Could they be keeping their options open in the hope of getting a better offer? Perish the thought, but it is an easy conclusion to draw. So don't be tardy if you're invited (word gets around).

Formal invitations still to this day are correctly replied to in the third person.

Mr Alasdair Franks thanks Mr Peter Moore for his kind invitation to dinner on Friday, 12 November at half-past seven at The Gables and has much pleasure in accepting/regrettably cannot attend.

The date of your response is then written underneath. Signing your name as well is a major gaffe and you will be exposed as an imposter if you do so. Obviously you can't sign your acceptance anyway on an email, unless you sign the original response form, scan it, convert it into a pdf ... hell, life's too short. Buy a first-class stamp.

Invitations by telephone can be replied to there and then, although as a prospective guest do not be afraid to say you will have to check and telephone back – again, within a few days. As a host you should never put guests on the spot. Never use the telephone, unless you're inviting close friends or family (in which case you can legitimately retort to a qualified acceptance:

'Don't be ridiculous, you haven't got that many friends. And I don't care if you've been invited by Jay Gatsby, you're coming to me. No argument.')

Invitations sent by text are worse than invitations made by telephone and can be replied to in the same manner that they were issued (don't be surprised if it's a resounding no). But worst of all as a means of inviting and accepting, is to use a social networking service like Facebook. This removes any remnants of style and class by presenting the guest with three options: 'attending', 'maybe attending' and 'not attending'. Focus on that middle option for a moment, and then don't give your invitee a choice: no one is *maybe* attending anything. You are either going or you are not. If you are free and want to go, you click 'attending'; if you are free but don't want to go, or simply not free, then you are 'not attending'.

Once the guest has accepted a formal invitation, there's no turning back. Failing to turn up is simply not done, unless you come down with a highly contagious illness like ebola, or perhaps have to leave the country to stay one step ahead of an extraordinary rendition to Guantanamo. They should make sure their excuse is a good one, and offer profuse apologies and mean them.

HOSTESS GIFTS

Upon arrival at any form of event, it is incorrect to show up empty-handed. As a host you should say nothing, but put a mental black line through the guest's name. It is the correct form to bring a hostess gift (incidentally, it's described as such even if there isn't a hostess).

Unless the guests know your exact taste in wine then turning up with a bottle or two of end-of-bin bargains is best avoided – in some parts of the world it is taken as an insult to arrive with wine, because it implies that your hosts' wine cellar isn't good enough. A bottle of Champagne (*grand cru* naturally) and/or chocolates will suffice. They shouldn't be tempted to make the latter Ferrero Rocher; it wasn't funny the first time around.

Flowers may be presented although only if already in water (the correct term is actually 'aqua bouquet') – cut flowers with exposed stems will mean that you need to put them in water immediately. This is not what an already over-worked host wants to do. The more considerate and clever guest sends the flowers the day before, with a note attached saying how much they are looking forward to coming. You can then take longer to display them and many will be grateful for your contribution to the décor for the event. This trick is particularly useful for houseguests, who may be travelling a long way and do not have time to find any suitable hostess gift.

Hosts should react favourably to any gift that is presented to them, even if they hate it. There is always something to say without compromising common politeness.

Do say What a lovely thought. Would you mind if I opened it later?
Don't say No Ferrero Rocher, no entry.

The Japanese like to bring fine cuts of steak to each other's houses as a hostess gift, yet the practice of turning up with a decent chunk of top rump, however delicious it may prove to be, has not yet caught on in the West.

Any gift handed over to the hostess should not be expected to be seen again that evening by guests. So, as a hostess, don't be tempted to open it in front of your guests. It's just not done.

TOURING & SNOOPING

Never be tempted to offer to show your guests around your home. The only possible exception to this is if you have just moved into a new home and it has some particularly notable features and architectural quirks. A 110-inch Ultra HDTV television in the 'lounge' doesn't qualify. But a Banksy on the back wall does. 'Yes, it was indeed Banksy,' you might say, gesturing casually at a random scrawl in lurid red paint (which you'll have prepared earlier). 'He was here at a party a few months ago and we thought he was just having a cigarette in the garden. Apparently it's done no harm to the resale value.'

If you're entertaining at home, expect a critical appraisal of your décor, objets, artworks, books and furniture. If you have any snaps of yourself taken with notable public figures, it's not a bad idea to leave them discreetly on bookshelves, but sometimes it just makes more sense to hire a neutral venue where you can't be judged by your taste (or lack of it).

Bluffers hosting parties in particularly grand environs should remember not to show themselves up by gesturing excitedly at the Canaletto on the wall, or the pink Baccarat crystal chandeliers. Instead the attitude to be adopted should be one of studied indifference – after all, you must give the impression that chandeliers and Canalettos of this sort are your birthright. This should not be verbally expressed but silently signified by appropriate inscrutability as you acknowledge your guests' breathless admiration.

Do say 'I'm more of a fan of Guardi to be honest. I feel that, crucially, he emphasised the fragility of Venice rather than its permanence.'
Don't sing (to the tune of 'O Sole Mio') 'One Canaletto – give it to me. A Venetian artist from Italy. ...'

INTERACTING WITH STAFF
Staff are there to serve, but they should also be treated with due respect and not dismissed as mere functionaries. It is terribly bad form to be rude to them, but as a host you should ensure that they don't become over familiar. Guests should not flirt with them, and vice versa, and no-one in the serving staff should ever be seen with a drink raised to their lips, unless you – as host – suggest it as a reward when the last guest has gone.

Generally speaking, hosts and guests alike need not say 'thank you' every time a member of the serving staff performs some task around them, especially if they are engrossed in conversation. Make sure you do say thank you from time to time, however, and when leaving the table or party be sure to thank them then.

WORKING A ROOM

Don't hog any one guest. A key bluffing tip is make an impression quickly, hint at great depths of knowledge and expertise at whatever subject is being discussed, and move on before you're found out. As a rule of thumb this will be no more than ten minutes. The first rule of entertainment, in whatever guise it takes, is always to leave your audience wanting more. It's not hard to move on, and can be as easy as saying that you 'really must mingle'. Of course, you may not even be granted the full ten minutes with one particular guest, and might be surprised to discover that they're planning to move on themselves. In these circumstances, should you suspect that they're planning to make the first move, look over their shoulder and wave at an imaginary new arrival.

There's a good way of uncovering your guests' intentions: the position of their feet can be very telling if they've decided they want to move on, especially men's feet and women in flat shoes. If they are pointing at you, you're safe. If one foot is pointing towards the door, or another group of people, body language experts tell us that the chances are that this is the direction their brain is telling them they want to go. Look at the feet and learn to wrap the conversation up pronto – even if it involves walking away mid-sentence. It's do or die.

There will come a time, inevitably, when you are stuck with the party bore. They might be pleasant enough, but are guilty of the cardinal sin of possessing very little conversation, knowledge, wit or charm. You do not need to be stuck with them for longer than it takes to hand them over to some unsuspecting victim. This is how to do it.

You   Frank, it has been *so* interesting to catch up, but I've just seen someone over there [point vaguely at the other side of the room] who I must go and catch before they leave. Have you met Rosemary Rumpole, however? [You have spotted Rosemary standing on her own nearby.]

Frank   No, I haven't.

You   Right, well let me come and introduce you. I may be mistaken, but I think you might find that you share some family connections.

Frank   How intriguing.

You   [Guiding Frank towards Rosemary] Rosemary, hello again! May I introduce Frank Spencer? I think you two might find you have a lot in common.

Rosemary Oh really…?

You   So sorry again, Frank, Rosemary – I must now dash to catch George and Mary over there as I think they're about to leave but I'll see you both later.

You can then beat a speedy retreat and make sure you position yourself a safe distance away from both. It'll take them at least 20 minutes to discover that they have nothing in common whatsoever. Rosemary may not thank you, but she can use a similar tactic a few minutes into the conversation. It's Frank's fault for being boring but he must not be left standing on his own. Again, it cannot be emphasised enough at any social function which you might be hosting that guests should never be left standing on their own. People staring at their feet is not the sign of a good party.

CANDID CAMERA

If the party is taking place to mark a particular occasion, maybe a landmark birthday or a charity gala, then a photographer may be invited to record it. If you happen to see the photographer heading purposefully in your direction, then put the glass down. One of the unwritten rules about being a natural host or guest is never to be knowingly photographed holding a glass. This is almost as ill-advised as wearing a baseball cap, holding a banana, or eating a bacon sandwich. A candid shot of you across a room is acceptable, as you were unlikely to be aware that the photo was being taken, but a staged photograph is where you find the nearest surface and place down the glass for a short moment. The same rule applies to 'selfies', the pandemic infecting society where mobile phone users feel obliged to photograph anything of arguable interest happening to them and then post it on social media. If they demand that you should join them in a 'selfie' with them, look suitably puzzled or reluctant. That way your peers won't judge you too harshly when they see your picture later. And remember, put the glass down.

THANKS

Thank you letters are compulsory. If you fail to receive one, get out your black book, wield your black pen, and strike through the guest's name in black ink.

A thank you letter means just that. A thank you text, while better than nothing, is not the same thing. It simply doesn't carry the same cachet as a proper letter delivered by Royal Mail.

Guests should not expect a thank you letter back from their hosts to thank them for the hostess gift. Otherwise it could become a never-ending cycle of gratitude.*

RETURNING HOSPITALITY

The unwritten (until now) rule of entertaining is: you give, you receive. And if you receive, you give. Versatility is key and those who enjoy the hospitality of others are expected to return the favour within at least six months of the event … unless they wish to end the friendship.

*If you happen to find yourself entertaining some guests in Nigeria, earn maximum bluffing points for remembering that hosts are expected to write to the guests to thank them for attending their party.

WHAT'S YOUR POISON?

Remember, it's called a drinks party if there are no cocktails being served. This basic, and rather obvious, rule is often overlooked by many hosts who decide to host a cocktail party only for guests to find the most exotic drink on offer is Cava. Aspiring bluffers take note: if the invitation reads 'cocktail party' then cocktails are what your guests should expect to drink.

THE GENERAL FORM

Drinks or cocktail parties are a very practical way of entertaining a large number of people. In the world of entertaining, it is usually understood that by holding one of these you are not paying back dinner invitations. A dinner invitation can only be paid back in kind. All hosts know this, but not quite so many guests do.

Drinks parties are generally held over two or three hours during the evening, although many go on for much longer. On the invitation the host would normally never state the end time, just the start time. Guests are expected to know when to leave. A good rule of thumb is that if everyone else has gone, it is probably time for you to go too.

If you are hosting a drinks or cocktail party at your home, it is usually a sensible idea to put away any ornaments of financial, artistic, or sentimental value. Guests are notoriously careless around other people's possessions. Think carefully about potential trip-hazards, such as footstools, baskets, pets or children.

As a host you might be well advised not to get too carried away with the invitations. Smaller numbers work better – too many people and the guests will just feel like they're making up numbers. It's a fine balance; too few guests and you might risk a deafening silence. So you'll need enough people to create a buzz, but not so many that you'll begin to wonder who some of them are.

And never place the bar too close to the entrance, or the buffet (should you be having one) next to the bar. Think carefully about where both could be sited to ensure a smooth flow of guests finding their own space.

FASHIONABLY LATE

There is no such thing as 'fashionably late'. It's simply termed 'unforgiveably rude'. Arriving deliberately late is the height of bad manners and the few guests who do try to pull this stunt are misguided, having persuaded themselves that they bring so much sparkle and life to the party that they can get away with it. They are often mistaken.

For any sort of social entertaining, all guests should look to arrive 10 to 15 minutes after the specified time on the invitation. An invitation for lunch at 12.30 does not mean that food will be served then, it means that your guests can arrive *from* 12.30 (although, now you know that really this means 12.45 latest). The lunch itself will probably be served at 1.15, but certainly not until all the guests arrive. Should guests arrive any earlier than the designated time, or later than the 15-minute extension, then prepare to greet them warmly at the door while silently planning their social excommunication as you pour them their first drink.

There is no such thing as 'fashionably late'. It's simply termed 'unforgiveably rude'.

Business entertaining is different – breakfast, brunches, lunches, coffee dates and most dinners start on time, much like business meetings. So if a colleague agrees to meet at 3.30pm for tea, then 3.30pm exactly is when they should turn up. It would only be for evening meals in a client or colleague's house that the 10- to 15-minutes late rule would again be applicable.

Any delay in arrival should be communicated via a telephone call (not a text). You can then adjust your timings and make the decision to start serving those guests who are polite enough to have made it on time.

DRINKS

Hosts should plan on a minimum of four drinks per person, on the grounds that some will drink none and others will drink eight. One bottle of wine has about six 125ml glasses in it. Do the math, as our American friends say.

A basic offering for a drinks party:

- Red and white wine
- Champagne (or top notch sparkling)
- Sherry (dry to medium)
- Water (still and sparkling)
- Orange juice
- A cordial of some sort
- For more casual drinks parties – bottles of beer, possibly a barrel (or two).

COCKTAILS

Cocktail parties are more elaborate. Although preparing just one cocktail needs a lot of work, think twice before hiring a professional or two to mix them. Depending on the size of the guest list, you're almost certainly going to need more than that, and you will almost certainly find that you're paying 'professional mixologists' a not insignificant sum to show off by doing cringeworthy impressions of Tom Cruise in the 1980s film 'Cocktail' and flirting with your guests. The bluffer will benefit from making economies here, while simultaneously reducing the queues waiting for a drink. Simply limit the choice of cocktails to half a dozen classics (not including non-alcoholic versions) and invest in six 'cocktail shakers' (about £15 each from all good department stores). Some of them helpfully have the ingredients and measurements etched on the side. One bartender/

waiter mixes them, the other serves them. Stock up on plenty of ice, relevant fruit, and a few packs of cocktail accessories such as swizzle sticks and paper umbrellas, and get shakin'.

THE CLASSICS

Every good host should always have both the ingredients and the recipes to make at least a few good cocktails and there are certain essentials you should never be without. Of the traditional spirits, gin, whiskey and vodka are the most popular and can be served neat (except in the case of gin) and mixed. Start with those basic spirits and build your drinks cabinet up from there, adding vermouths, liqueurs and bitters as you go, as well as other popular spirits such as rum, brandy and tequila.

Cocktails can be something of a social booby-trap. Done properly and they can be sophisticated and elegant; done badly and they can be sticky, tacky and virtually undrinkable. Classics will include the Martini or Manhattan; by contrast, avoid serving anything called Sex on the Beach, Slippery Nipple or Screaming Orgasm – especially to the local rector.

This is the bluffer's choice of ten all-time great cocktails. Take your pick.

- **Bellini** – a truly elegant Prosecco-based cocktail made with peach purée. It was invented in Harry's Bar in Venice in the 1930s. You might comment knowledgeably that the Pink Bellini (made with a touch of raspberry juice) was popularised by the late broadcaster Alan Whicker who found any excuse to be filmed drinking one while propping up a bar in a blazer and cravat.

- **Bloody Mary** – arguably the world's most complex cocktail, a vodka and tomato juice-based mixture which is a must for any self-respecting brunch party. You will know that it has eight ingredients, sometimes eleven if going the whole hog (although you can leave out the clam juice and dash of sherry, but not the celery salt and Worcester sauce). A 'Virgin Mary' is the same cocktail without the vodka. And to be honest, the only way to tell the difference is if you're still standing after four of them.

- **Champagne Cocktail** – a simple and classic aperitif, requiring only Champagne, a touch of Cognac, a sugar cube and some bitters. There is little point in using an expensive Champagne, so save that for the toast.

- **Daiquiri** – leaving aside its damagingly high number of name checks in the Tom Cruise film (which you will say was utterly vacuous) the Daiquiri is a classic rum drink with many variations, but mainly mixed with lime juice.

- **Manhattan** – among the all-time great cocktails, it is a mixture of whisky and sweet vermouth. Don't forget the Angostura bitters.

- **Margarita** – one of the most instantly recognisable cocktails thanks to the salt-rimmed glass in which it is served, and one of the few quality tequila drinks that you are permitted to be seen drinking in public (unlike, for example, a 'Tequila Sunrise').

- **Martini** – the most classic of the cocktails. Martinis are made with gin unless stated otherwise. Vodka is an acceptable, though less traditional alternative. The other main ingredient is dry vermouth, but not too much; Noel Coward once famously said: the ideal Martini should be made by 'filling a glass with gin then waving it in the general direction of Italy'.
- **Mojito** – a popular and refreshing mint-infused rum drink. Make sure you have an extensive supply of mint sprigs if you plan on making them for a party. Never make the mistake of thinking that Mojito is Spanish for mosquito. In fact the cocktail's name comes from the verb 'mojar' – to wet, or moisten.
- **Old Fashioned** – the definitive 'early' cocktail. American whiskey, sugar syrup, water and bitters. It should be served in a low-ball glass, garnished with lemon peel and maraschino cherry. You'll be looking like Don Draper in no time.
- **Sidecar** – a mixture of Cointreau or triple sec, lemon juice, Cognac or Armagnac, its origins can be traced to The Ritz in Paris.

Do Say What your desired choice of gin is for your martini. A muscular gin like Tanqueray is suitable for dry martinis, whereas a more botanical brand like Bombay Sapphire works well for those who like their vermouth.

Don't Say 'Shaken not stirred'. Leaving aside the fact that any barman will have heard this a thousand times, it is also a universally rejected means of preparing a Martini. Shaking the drink merely breaks the ice, thus overly diluting it. All bluffers must know this.

FOOD

Canapés are the order of the evening, for both forms of party. These are held in the fingers, and generally eaten in one bite. The rule is eight to ten canapés per guest. You might want to hire in caterers to help you with this, because it's both time consuming and largely unrewarding making your own selection of pigs in a blanket (that's a cocktail sausage wrapped in bacon) and angels on horseback (that's an oyster wrapped in bacon, obviously). Of your offering have about five or six hot ones and two or three cold. Ensure that there is a reasonable balance between meat- and vegetable-based varieties.

Whatever is served must be eaten in one, maybe two mouthfuls. If it involves a cocktail stick, instruct your serving staff to wait until the canapé has been safely delivered into the guest's mouth so that they're not left standing holding a toothpick.

Don't Say They're from Iceland's premium range. Awfully good value.

GATECRASHERS

You must decide your policy on gatecrashers before the party. Either let them in, or ask them to leave. People turning up who are not invited and you don't know are technically guilty of a crime if they consume your food and drink (it's called theft) and need to be removed. People you do know but were not invited are guilty of an even worse offence (social transgression). Try to avoid making too much of a fuss when asking them to leave.

GETTING GUESTS OUT OF THE KITCHEN

Some guests think it is their duty to 'entertain' you by following you into the kitchen and generally distracting you. As well meaning as they might be, having too many people in a place of food preparation can be a nuisance. Some tactics you might adopt to get rid of them include:

- Give them jobs that involve them working outside the kitchen, such as taking the rubbish out, or asking them to check everyone has a drink, or that the loos haven't run out of lavatory paper, maybe even to make sure that the next door neighbour who doesn't know anybody has someone to talk to.

- Make sure the drinks and food are not out on display or on offer in the kitchen. Place them as far away as possible in other rooms, otherwise they will act like a magnet to kitchen squatters.

- Before the party, get some yellow tape and mark out a zone in the kitchen where you can, faux-bossily, tell guests they must not cross or feel your wrath. If they come across it, bark, 'behind the line!'

- Perhaps the best solution is to make the rest of your reception rooms as appealing as the kitchen. When a guest arrives, lead them to a room with others, introduce them, get them a drink, make sure the canapés are *en route* and ensure they are comfortable with that environment. If they are, they will probably stay there. Some guests never move.

ß

'If it's rissoles, I shan't dress – a rule I made in 1929 and to which I strictly adhere.'

(*Noël Coward*)

DRESSING THE PART

What you wear, more to the point, what you ask your guests to wear, is an important part of the whole entertaining caboodle. Wherever possible it is advisable to put the emphasis on 'smart casual' – and that way nobody will be disappointed. But there will always be occasions when it will be necessary, and actually rather refreshing, to expect guests to make a bit of an effort. And if they're expected to, so will you.

EVENING DRESS

Anyone wishing to enter the minefield of dress codes must know the difference between '*full* evening dress' and plain 'evening dress'. The answer is that the former means what is now termed as 'white tie' and the latter is 'black tie'. Unless you're planning a very grand occasion, it's best to avoid this end of the dress code scale. It's not really bluffing territory, so don't go there unless you're just planning to talk about it (which is what bluffers do best). So the best advice is, know about it, discuss it, but don't do it. This is what you need to know:

For full evening dress (white tie), men wear black cut-away tailcoats with matching trousers (with two pieces of braid down the side of each leg), stiff white dress shirts with winged collars, white marcella waistcoats, patent leather laced shoes and of course the white bow tie. Ladies need to wear dresses 'to the floor'. In its strictly correct sense this means longer dresses stopping just before the floor starts.

For evening dress (black tie), men wear a black or midnight blue dinner jacket (single or double-breasted is fine) with white turndown collar dress shirt, trousers matching the material and colour of the jacket but with one piece of braid running down them, black waistcoats or cummerbunds (pleats facing upwards) patent leather pumps and a black bow tie. Injecting colour, such as a red bowtie, is never wise and may lead to the offender being rightly ostracised. Women have more of a problem with black tie and should take their lead from the invitation and what style of event it is. A drinks party is usually fine for the LBD, but a sit-down dinner will need a grander dress that allows for the inevitable expansion as the food is consumed.

(For more detailed instruction on formal dress codes, including Morning Dress, refer to *The Bluffer's Guide to Etiquette*.)

FANCY DRESS

The British have a penchant for dressing up in costume, but those who will happily don white tie/black tie without a second thought, will dig their heels in when asked to wear a different sort of 'fancy' costume. It is safe to assume that the reverse is also true.

When the invitation bearing the challenging words 'fancy dress' arrives your guests have three options:

1. Decline to attend, pretending they are out of the country, visiting an infirm relative, suffering from a highly contagious disease, or dead.
2. Decide to attend, pulling no punches as regards costume. Half measures are not what are needed here. Their outfit must suit the occasion and the person.
3. Attend, but on their terms. This usually means making no effort at all, which is very bad form.

As a host, you will need to know that guests are made up of those who are easy to entertain and will fling themselves at full tilt into any theme or dress style, and those who stand sniffily aside implying that dressing up is demeaning (or simply not cool). In those circumstances you might think that there's not much the bluffer can do, but the good news is that there is. Choose a theme which can involve as little or as much effort as the guest wants to put into it. A good example is Bow Ties & Tiaras. Your male guests can turn up as James Bonds, or Chippendales, or just men in bow ties and T-shirts. Women can go the whole hog as Audrey Hepburn in a ballgown, or Miss World contestants, or just female guests in pound-store sparkly hair bands. To avoid any confusion regarding the flexibility of this particular dress code you must use the term 'bow tie' –

which means anything from a spinning novelty item to a cowboy lariat.

'With my sunglasses on I'm
Jack Nicholson.
Without them I'm fat and 60.'

Another simple theme is just 'sunglasses'. Don't be surprised if most of the women come as Jackie Onassis or Audrey Hepburn (note, as above, that her distinctive style is easily mimicked). Most of the men are likely to come as Elvis, Bono, or Jack Nicholson. (The latter, bluffers will drop adroitly into conversation, once famously said: 'With my sunglasses on I'm Jack Nicholson. Without them I'm fat and 60.')

Demonstrate your wisdom as a host by making the choice of fancy dress as easy as possible for your guests.

TOPPING STUFF

There's nothing easier than asking your guests to wear a hat. If you really must insist on a sartorial theme, your guests will thank you for making a hat the extent of the effort they are required to go to. Hats are not as ubiquitous as they once were, and more's the pity. But given any excuse for wearing one, most people seize the opportunity with alacrity.

But there are rules nonetheless and you will underline your bluffing credentials by having a passing acquaintance with them if you're holding a hat party:

For the ladies …
1. Avoid fascinators. There is nothing fascinating about fascinators. A proper hat will always trump something that looks like a bird which has flown into someone's head at high speed and is feebly waving a tail feather.
2. Formally, hats are not worn after 6pm. After that, it's tiara time. All rules are suspended, however, at a hat party.
3. Straw hats are only to be worn after Easter. Before that (or after September) then it's fabric hats only.
4. When attending a wedding or funeral, it is bad form to have a brim so wide that people in the rows behind cannot see what's going on ahead. This is also true of Wimbledon.
5. Ladies hats are often at an angle and are higher on their left and lower on their right.

For the chaps …
1. The fedora or homburg has a certain timeless appeal. Think Bogart or Indiana Jones. All men's hats should be at a slightly jaunty angle.
2. Men should always remove hats indoors. Unless, as above, they're at a party which permits one.
3. Men over 25 should never wear a baseball cap, unless they're at a baseball game. It has two effects – it can either permanently destroy your credibility or get you elected to the highest office in America.
4. Men under 25 should never wear a classic hat, especially a Panama.

BAL MASQUÉ

Masked balls effectively originated in Italy during the 16th century Renaissance. Any bluffer holding such an event must know this very basic of facts. Other European countries then adopted them, sometimes with fatal consequences – Gustav III of Sweden was assassinated during one in Stockholm in 1792 (you should also know that this unfortunate event was later turned into Verdi's opera 'Un ballo in maschera'/'A Masked Ball'). His assassins didn't make it easy for themselves – after all, it helps if you know who you're shooting. Fortunately for them Gustav presented himself as an easy target by wearing an enormous breast star signifying his membership of the Royal Order of the Seraphim (only available to Swedish kings). This was the equivalent of wearing a flashing neon sign reading 'Aim Here'.

Etiquette can vary at the masked balls of the 21st century, and it is obviously not the done thing to murder anyone, but if in doubt about the rules, make enquiries ahead of time. Guests are expected to keep their masks on all night, sometimes just until midnight, helping to protect their anonymity (although it is usually fairly obvious who is who if you know any of the guest list). As for what else is worn, masks aside, the dress code is usually some form of evening dress. But a good bluffer will relax the rules in this respect.

Masked balls are usually the scene of a lot of flirting, with guests sometimes surprised to find that they're attracted to someone actually without seeing their face. That, in fact, is the whole point of the masquerade, to prove that true beauty lies behind the ineffaceable mask that most people are stuck with.

The size and shape of the mask depends on how elaborate the party is (if you commit the cardinal sin of sending the invitation via text then don't expect your guests to go to town on their face furniture), but if your invitation is embossed and engraved to within an inch of its life then you are entitled to expect your guests to go all out with their masks.

Venetian-style masked balls require masks that cover the full face, otherwise it is advisable to stick to a half mask if you want your guests to have a relatively easy passage between hand and mouth when eating or imbibing.

SMART CASUAL

This dress code is a little unclear with many not knowing whether they can or cannot wear denim. Yes is the answer. Jeans are probably acceptable, so long as they are relatively smart, free from designer tears and rips, and worn correctly around the waist and not slung around the lower buttocks. And if older male guests want to wear chinos with their shirts out (a sure sign that their waist measurement is larger than their chest), then fine.

The tried and tested smart casual look for men is linen or cotton jacket in the summer, wool, cord or tweed in the winter. These can be worn with an open collar (just the one button unfastened, two only if on the continent). This can be dressed up or down accordingly. Smart casual for women also generally requires some form of jacket or top, which can be worn with skirt or smart trousers. Leggings are best left at home, or better still, in the shop.

The key for guests is to make sure they look like they've changed and made at least some sort of effort. They don't need to have dressed in their finest togs, as the name suggests, but it is very different from 'come as you are'. …

COME AS YOU ARE

This is not to be taken literally by your guests. It is a synonym for 'dress casually' but does not give licence for guests to arrive in the same soiled trousers they've been wearing to tend to their perennials all day. Jeans and crisp shirts or ironed T-shirts are fine; smarter shorts in the summer months are also passable. Women may show off a lean and depilated expanse of bare leg.

SHOES ON OR OFF

One of the biggest dilemmas in entertaining is the issue of whether you should ask your guests to remove their shoes on arrival at your home. There is a simple answer to this: don't. It suggests that you have an unhealthy and fastidious approach to cleanliness which is unlikely to be conducive to a relaxed occasion. If a no-shoes policy isn't a requirement at any of The Queen's official residences, or at the most exclusive clubs, hotels and restaurants in the country, then it shouldn't be a requirement at your own slightly less exalted address. If you're worried about the brand new cream Axminster getting soiled, the best advice is to cover it with something (not a good look), or get a new carpet, or find a different venue.

Next you'll be telling your guests that there isn't a smoking area on or near the premises, in which case you really shouldn't think about entertaining at home.

UNHELPFUL DRESS CODES

Sadly, some hosts have an increasing propensity to re-invent the wheel when it comes to dress codes. They pepper their invitations with phrases such as 'upscale casual', 'semi-formal', 'black tie with a hint of inner child'. These may make sense to the host but presenting guests with a challenge before they have even arrived at the party is plain bad manners and not playing fair. If you're tempted do this, don't be surprised if guests faced with a problem dress code then telephone you to seek clarification. Effectively they're questioning your hosting skills. And they have a point.

'We've both had days where it was either set a beautiful table, or curl up in a ball and die.'

(Katherine Mayfair, Desperate Housewives)

DRINKING & DINING DECORUM

An elegant, formal dinner is one of the most effective ways to commemorate a special occasion, and a properly set table will get you off to a good start. If you're aiming to seriously impress your guests the key elements must all be in place, from sparkling lead crystal goblets to perfectly polished silverware and the starchiest linens, to place settings measured with military precision. There is a big measure of theatre involved in holding a formal dinner, indeed the table is as important as the food, but it helps if you get the balance right and don't focus too much on one to the detriment of the other. The secret as far as presentation is concerned is to ensure that everything is in the right place – frilly touches such as rose petals, silver-sprayed birch twigs and individual lanterns are all very well, but nothing surpasses a table that is correctly set. It makes a clear point that the host has put themselves out on their guests' behalf.

A proper place setting should be perfectly balanced and equidistant from each neighbour. In the most exalted dining circles tables are painstakingly measured with a ruler for accurate spacing, and settings should always be in line with a table centrepiece.

Give your full attention to the following:

TABLECLOTH OR TABLEMATS

Decide on whether you want to use a crisp tablecloth, or cork or felt-backed tablemats. It is one or the other; never both. Traditionally, cloths were always used. These days many hosts choose to show the French-polished wood and so opt for mats. If tablemats are to be used, they should be an inch away from the edge of the table and positioned carefully parallel to it with the design facing the diner.

CENTREPIECE

Place the centrepiece next, so that cutlery and glasses can be arranged geometrically around it. It can be a flower arrangement, a tray of festive candles, an Easter Egg tree, a sculpture, or even a bowl of retro sweets (naturally the bowl will be the finest crystal). If flowers are used make sure they are small and low – a bristling hedge of miniature leylandii down the middle of the table will just annoy guests and block the view.

CUTLERY

Lower edges of cutlery are aligned with the bottom edge of the main plate, which is about half an inch away from the edge of the table.

It is important for bluffers to know that all cutlery is set by holding it from the point of balance. On a fork this is where the bridge meets the handle; the same is true for spoons. Knives are held from where the blade meets the handle.

Cutlery is set and used in the order of use: working from the outside, inwards. Thus, for a simple three-course meal, if the first course is melon and Parma ham, a small fork and knife will be the cutlery set furthest away from the dinner plate, and next would come the cutlery for the main course, followed by the pudding fork and spoon.

Because most people are right-handed (and indeed being a leftie was once seriously frowned upon) right-handed settings are the norm. This means knives and spoons on the right, and forks on the left. Today we are much more tolerant of the left-handed (they are often much cleverer than right-handed people) but there is no need to switch the setting for them. They can simply pick up the relevant fork in their left and corresponding knife or spoon in the right and switch for each course.

Knives are set with their blades facing the plate – away from harm. If the opportunity arises point out that this is a custom that dates back to the Middle Ages when an outwards pointing blade indicated that the diner was ready for combat (but not over pudding when the only weapon is a spoon).

The bread knife or butter spreader is set either down the side with the rest of the knives (on the outermost side), or – as is modern practice – actually on the bread plate.

Don't show your naivety by not knowing which is the only fork set on the right-hand side of the plate. It, is of course, the Oyster fork (but you knew that). That said, serving oysters at a dinner party isn't really the done thing unless you are a footballer's wife.

In traditional British settings, no cutlery is ever placed above the dinner plate, although this custom seems to be fast on the way out. Above the place setting you may instead see a crescent-shaped salad plate, although this practice has gone so far out it won't ever come back. While it would be preferable for all cutlery to be placed along the side of the plate, if space is tight then it is now permissible to place the pudding cutlery above with the spoon above the fork; this style is called 'nursery' (as it was only seen in the children's nurseries). When in use the spoon handle should face right and the fork handle should face left, with the spoon above the fork. But if you happen to be hosting aristocracy or royalty, then show that you are basically 'one of them' by not adopting the nursery position. You might even be rewarded with an admiring comment.

When setting the table, it is generally advisable to use cotton gloves to ensure that no fingermarks are left on cutlery. Remember to take them off when the guests arrive, or they might think you've got a nasty skin condition.

PLATES

As previously indicated, the main plates are set about half an inch in from the table edge, and in the centre of the setting. If you are using a service plate (also known as a 'charger') then these are the exception and are aligned flush with the edge of the table, although not traditionally seen in British settings.

The bread plate goes to the left of the setting. In Britain, it is aligned with the bottom of the main plate. In American settings, it is set in the top left of the setting (cover), above the forks.

NAPKINS

Napkins are set in the space where the dinner plate will go or on the side plate. On no account should paper napkins be used at a formal dinner. Instead opt for plain linen or linen damask. Cotton will suffice if all else fails.

Very elaborately folded napkins can look overdone, and modern practice is to leave flat on the side plate. However, a fold such as the Bishops' Mitre or Prince of Wales plume are acceptable. But don't do a swan, and never place the napkins in a glass.

SALT, PEPPER & OTHER CONDIMENTS

Condiments are placed at regular intervals between place settings. At very grand dinners there may be a set for each individual place. Salt and pepper pots (mills are acceptable only at informal occasions) should be parallel to each other with the mustard in front. If there is no mustard pot, then the salt should be placed in front of the pepper. Relish or chutney must be served in a sauceboat with ladle and, if you value your future as a host of taste and good breeding, never place a bottle of ketchup on the table. Even at brunch.

If finger food is being served, a finger bowl is set to the left, above the forks. Sliced lemon is sometimes used to cut through any residual grease. Extra bluffing points if you point out the water you put in these is cold because of course you'll know that hot water will open the pores in the fingers and allow the smell of the food to penetrate the skin and prove difficult to get rid of.

GLASSES

Place glasses last, at the right hand of the setting just above the dinner knife and arrange them from front to back in the order in which they will be used. The water glass (often the same size of glass used for red wine or in more modern settings a water goblet) is placed slightly behind and on the left of the wine glasses.

It is no longer customary to have masses of matching glasses. White wine is generally served in narrower glasses than red, for which a more rounded shape is usually preferred. At table, Champagne should be served in flutes and not the old-fashioned coupes (fine for a drinks party), although that is by no means a hard and fast rule.

Drinks mats or coasters should never be used, no matter how precious the table wood.

Make sure glasses are set by holding the stems, rather than the bowl or rim as this will leave off-putting fingermarks.

FILLING THEM

Preprandial drinks (always call them 'aperitifs') are the traditional way to preface dinner, and they enable people to greet each other, break the ice and dip in and out of conversations before they are seated. They also allow the host to do a swift circuit of the room and make sure that everyone has been properly welcomed.

The purpose of aperitifs is to stimulate the appetite and prepare the body for food. They're also useful for encouraging conversation and setting the tone of the meal. Since aperitifs are by definition a transition to another activity, stick to small glasses to keep things moving and regulate intake. It helps if your guests are still relatively sober during the main course, so stay strong and focus on quality not quantity.

A timeless favourite is a pale, dry Amontillado sherry. Other fail-safe aperitifs include Champagne as well as crisp, minerally whites like Grüner Veltliner and Albariño. And don't forget the drivers and teetotallers – have something more interesting than mineral water to offer them.

Guests should avoid the 'provinces out for a country house hotel Sunday lunch look' and must never take their aperitif glasses through to the dining room.

PAIRING & POURING

The problem of pairing wine and food seems to be a source of anxiety to many hosts. It doesn't need to be if you follow two basic rules. Firstly, it's far more important to pair wines with people's preferences, not the food. Secondly, wine and food in general work well together – there are only a few combinations that really don't work, despite what wine snobs say.

If you know that your guest drinks nothing else but a bold meaty claret, then don't be afraid to offer it with fish. Similarly, if their tipple is a fresh and fruity Riesling, then feel free to serve it up with a good steak.

Rules are made to be broken, and bluffers break more than most.

SOME TIPS:

- Try a different wine with each course (space, wine glasses and budget allowing).
- If you have a very special wine (preferably a case of it), design the food around the wine.
- Remember that food tends to dominate the wine and not vice versa.
- White wines should be served gently chilled (not fresh from a domestic fridge), ideally around 12°C.
- Red wines should be served *'chambre'*, or room temperature. Uncork well in advance (a couple of hours). If your red wine is too cold, a quick blast in the microwave at full heat will help (but don't admit this to your guests). And don't forget to unscrew it first, or take the cork out (in case you forget it's in there. An exploded bottle of red wine doesn't really set quite the right tone.)
- Use a decanter with a gauze cloth and funnel for mature wines to remove sediment before serving.
- Serving wines in the bottle used to be a major faux pas but it is now perfectly acceptable. Especially when it has an interesting label (you might think about using fake self-adhesive ones, especially those which purport to show that the wine is from your own vineyard).
- Allow one glass per person for each course. At the very minimum.*

*See The Bluffer's Guide to Wine for a pithy introduction to a subject which is sometimes needlessly over-complicated.

When at table, drinks are served from the right-hand side of the diner (those with any basic service training will be on the lookout for this), which is where you will find the glasses. Serving them from the left entails leaning unceremoniously across the diner and is best avoided.

There is no need to rotate the bottle after pouring each glass unless it is a very old bottle with sediment – but there's no harm in rotating anyway. It gives the impression that it's second nature to drink fine old vintages.

DIGESTIFS

These are postprandial drinks which should be offered at the end of the meal. This final, liquid course offers a soft landing and can settle the stomach after a heavy meal. Set a tray or trundle up a trolley with an array of small glasses and a variety of liqueurs. Vary the spirits by colour (crème de violette, yellow chartreuse, ruby port … or, if you really want to show off, white port), flavour/texture (sweet, herbal, creamy), and potency, and encourage your guests to share around. Or, consider the communal bottle and uncork a sipping gem (Madeira, Armagnac, malt whisky) for a more contemplative mood. After a full menu of cocktails, dinner wines and pudding wine look to keep the volumes smaller but the flavours intensified. And don't forget the coffee (including something utterly pointless called 'decaffeinated'.)

'Nobody looks back on their life and remembers the nights they got plenty of sleep.'

(Anon)

PARTY GAMES

The best form of entertainment at any type of party is invariably animated, interesting and spirited conversation. But, sometimes, parties need a bit of a lift. It may just be an unfortunate case of the dynamic being not quite right. If so, it could be time for a party game.

But one thing needs to be clear from the outset. Charades are never acceptable. No one really enjoys them except the person who bossily suggests them and nothing is more certain to kill any fun than fastidious explanations of intricate rules.

And before suggesting any party game, make sure you know your market: Aunt Maud is never going to be up for sardines, and any suggestion to the Apostolic Nuncio that he joins you for a quick round of Cards Against Humanity is just pure bad taste. Context matters, too. Are you sure your guests are in need of stimulation after a big lunch? However entertaining, any game that is overly physical or that requires strenuous movement (such as 'Twister') isn't going to be universally welcomed.

Whatever the game, the key to success is to be able to explain it in as few sentences as possible. If people don't understand every nuance and rule in advance then it doesn't matter. It's a game! They can learn as they go, as long as they grasp the basic concept. And learning can actually be part of the fun.

Another key guideline for any game is never to take it too seriously. By the time any party game has ended, the only desired result is for the players to be laughing. Whether the rubric has been followed to the letter is not really that relevant.

SEDENTARY GAMES

Consequences
The players sit in a circle and are each given a sheet of writing paper and a pen. At the top of the piece of paper, in a line, they write one or two adjectives. The piece of paper is then folded over so that what has been written cannot be seen. Every player then passes their piece of paper to the right. Everyone then writes down a gentleman's name, folds the paper over and passes it on – again to the right. The process continues until everyone has written, in order:

One or two adjectives
The name of a gentleman present
One or more adjectives
The name of a lady present
Where they met

What he gave to her
What he said to her
What she said to him
The consequence
What the world said.

Remember to fold down the piece of paper with each round. When everyone has done all this, the papers are collected and a spokesman proceeds to read out the various papers. As an example, an end result can read something like this: 'The engaging and gentle (1) Roger (2) met the voluptuous (3) Jennifer (4) in Macarthur Park (5); he gave her his screwdriver (6) and said to her, 'They don't make them like that anymore, dear' (7). She said to him, 'That'll loosen up my potato salad,' (8). And the consequence was they won the hot-dog eating championship (9) and the world said, 'You can see why more and more people are going vegan' (10).

Musical spoons
Like musical chairs but for the more immobile or inert. Count out one spoon per person in the party, remove one, and arrange the remainder in a circle either on the floor or on a table. All the players kneel, stand or sit around the circle. Music is played and when it is stopped everyone attempts to grab a spoon from the circle, and the person who is left empty handed is eliminated from the game. Remember to remove one spoon at the end of each round. Beware false fingernails, many of which are like claws and guaranteed to leave deep gouges if the game becomes very competitive (which it will).

Never have I ever
This can either be played as a seated drinking game or with everyone standing. One participant declares something that they have never done. Every member of the party who has also not done what has just been said either sits down or takes a sip of their drink. Those that have remain standing/do not drink. For example: 'Never have I ever been to Burnley' or 'Never have I ever had a gin and Dubonnet' or 'Never have I ever phoned in sick at work' and so on. The game can get predictably riotous when players are 'called out' for being economical with the truth.

Who am I?
On a sticky note or Post-It, each player writes down the name of a famous character or person that they're sure will be familiar to the player on their right. This is then securely affixed to that person's forehead. Each participant then tries to figure out which famous person they are by asking only 'Yes' or 'No' questions to gain clues about their identity. 20 questions maximum, and the winner is the first person to guess who they are correctly.

A LITTLE LIGHT MOVEMENT

The feather game
Players sit in a close circle and someone throws a feather into the air. By frantic, furious blowing, each puffing player tries to keep the feather away from them. Whoever the feather lands on incurs a forfeit.

Flap the kipper

A deceptively competitive game, distinguished by a high level of stamina and determination. There are two teams, and one player from each propels a cut-out, fish-shaped piece of paper around a marked circuit on the floor by fanning or flapping their 'kipper' with a newspaper or magazine of equal size, shape and weight. To ensure there is no unfair advantage conferred by 'inside tracks', players start from opposite ends and pass in the middle (which can be entertaining in itself). Contact between the kipper and the player flapping it results in instant disqualification.

Muddled string

Find as many different, distinctively coloured balls of wool as there are people in your party. Unroll each one, in and around the furniture. The winner is the first person to roll their wool back into a ball. Tip: remove all Sèvres vases first.

Make 'em laugh

Divide the party into two teams and seat the members of each team facing each other. The idea is that team A has to make team B laugh using physical contortions, peculiar noises, gurning, rude gestures – but no talking. Team B has to keep as many straight faces as possible. If someone cracks a smile in team B then they join team A and help to break the remaining players in team B. The winner is the last one not smiling. Then the teams reset and team A have to keep straight faces.

Pass the Orange

Physically intimate game where players line up in teams of four or more. Each team is equipped with an orange. The first player wedges it under his or her chin and attempts to pass it to the next player under their chin and so on. When the orange reaches the end of the line, the process is reversed. Hands are strictly forbidden, and if the orange is dropped, the player must go back to the start. Surprisingly entertaining.

Paper aeroplanes

Each player gets an A4 piece of paper and has to fold it into their best attempt at a paper aeroplane, with a wing (or wings) – thus no spherical shapes are permitted. Players then stand in a line and on one command launch their planes into the air. The plane which lands the furthest from the launch point wins. The best of five adds an extra element of competition, but modifications to the original model are not allowed.

Musical sleuths

This popular old parlour game requires the presence of a piano or keyboard, and one of the guests to be a reasonably proficient pianist. A small object is picked; one person (the sleuth) leaves the room and the others hide the object within that room. When the player returns the pianist performs a musical commentary on his or her proximity to the hidden object playing louder and building up the suspense as they draw near the object and softer as they move away. Set a time limit of 2 minutes per sleuth to add some jeopardy and to keep things from becoming dull. Keep score of the time each sleuth takes for each object, and the player who found their object the quickest wins. A good game for all ages, but especially for children (of all ages).

Ring of string
Take a small curtain ring, or napkin ring (the best use for the infernal items) or any other sort of ring. Thread a long piece of string through it and tie the two ends together to make a circle. Someone is elected 'it' and stands in the middle of the 'ring of string'. The remaining players then step inside the ring, keeping as close to each other as possible. With the string held behind their backs, the ring is passed continuously from player to player along the string while 'it' has to guess who they think has it. Players who don't have the ring can bluff and pretend to pass it to one another, hopefully prompting a false accusation from the guesser. As soon as they do guess correctly, they join the circle and the person who had the ring becomes 'it'. As ever, a limit on the number of guesses and/or a time limit helps to inject an element of competition.

These are just some suggestions. Asking your assembled guests to suggest their own games and entertainments is always a good option and makes the party uniquely memorable. And, remember, anyone who consistently wins hasn't really understood the point.

'I'm sitting here, waiting for death, serving tea to friends.'

(*Kenneth Williams*)

TEA TO A T

Thanks to Mary Berry, among others, afternoon tea is very much back in vogue. Social media is awash with snaps of people holding their teacups (pinkies extended, absurdly) and gorging on scones and tea-cakes. Tea appeals to all social classes, from the manual worker who prefers it as something to moisten his sugar, to the dowager countess for whom it is an elaborate ceremony involving warming pots, strainers and rules about adding milk. Whoever is drinking it, the occasion now known as 'afternoon tea' remains one of the most civilised and pleasurable ways to entertain friends and family. One of the principal advantages of hosting such an occasion is that it only need last a few hours or less; your guests are usually gone by 6pm, and you have the evening to yourself. But do not be fooled into thinking that this form of entertaining needs any less effort and attention than a dinner party. Finger sandwiches can be fiddly and are labour intensive, and getting your scones and lemon sponge to rise can be a challenge for novice bakers. But not for bluffers, because you will have had your local patisserie on the case all morning. Why waste time making it all yourself? There are far more important things to do (like completing the research on your guests).

First and foremost, you should be clear about the following: afternoon tea is *not* the same as high tea. Many, incorrectly, call sandwiches and scones 'high tea' as they think this sounds grander than just 'tea'. This is very wrong. Those in the know will not say anything, of course, but eyebrows will be raised. High tea was what children and staff of a large house ate in the early evenings, after the upstairs had been given their (afternoon) tea. It wasn't cucumber sandwiches. It was things like large joints of meat (often a roasted ham), slices of thick bread, potted shrimps, a big cake to share, and ale. It was eaten at a proper table, rather than a lower, coffee table, and so it became known in the servants' hall as 'high tea'. Later, for people staying in post-war, pre-package holiday British hotels and boarding houses it usually comprised sausage, egg and chips (distinguished from breakfast by the absence of fried bread). There are no signs that this particular menu is enjoying a resurgence in popularity.

It is generally believed that a woman of privilege called Anna Maria Russell, the seventh Duchess of Bedford, is the person to thank for introducing the tradition of afternoon tea. Back in the early 19th century meals were much further apart than they are now. The upper classes would eat dinner around 8.30pm, and maybe slightly later. Understandably, the duchess frequently became a little peckish in the middle of the afternoon and so ordered her servants to bring her some bread, jam & tea. As she sat alone, consuming this in her husband's ancestral seat of Woburn Abbey (pronounced Wooburn not Woe-burn) in Bedfordshire, she decided she'd much prefer to share the moment with her friends. So carriages from neighbouring estates rolled up, ladies gracefully alighted, and the idea caught on.

What then happened was that the newly created middle classes adopted the practice as well. But because they didn't have sprawling houses with sitting rooms or conservatories to entertain guests for tea, they created teahouses instead, the first of which in 1864 was the 'Aerated Bread Company' better known as 'The ABC tea house', which opened a number of branches in London and was the first fast food outlet of its day. Then the Lyons tea shop chain was established in 1884 and dominated the market for many years, opening its first famous 'Cornerhouse' in 1909. These were huge establishments arranged over many floors, with hairdressers, chocolate shops, theatre ticket booking agencies, themed restaurants, and of course the tea rooms themselves.

If you find yourself in a discussion about teahouses you can comment knowledgeably that the original ABC tearoom in London's Fenchurch Street station is now a Tesco Express. And although both ABCs and the cornerhouses have long since disappeared into the mists of time, the tradition of going out for afternoon tea is flourishing in Britain's smarter hotels and specialist tea shops. Don't expect to get change from £50 per person from the former.

What you must know is that in the world of entertaining, especially if you're bluffing about your extensive knowledge of the art, is that afternoon tea is not just a social occasion but – increasingly – a business one. If you're interviewing for, or being interviewed for, a job, you might well find yourself in the elegant environs of a hotel's palm court peering over the rim of a tea cup.

SANDWICHES

The sandwich is a staple dish of afternoon tea. You'll need to know something about their provenance if you plan to serve them, or order them, because the subject invariably crops up. It's a familiar story but it would take a brave bluffer to discount it. All you need to know is that it was invented by one John Montagu, the 4th Earl of Sandwich and the man who went on to become First Lord of the Admiralty. Montagu was an inveterate gambler who was so glued to the card table he started to miss meals. Eventually he ordered his staff to bring him some salt beef between two slices of bread – the bread was there to keep his hands clean so he could handle the cards without them sticking to his fingers. Interestingly, his ancestor Edward, the 1st Earl of Sandwich is thought to have wanted to be made Earl of Portsmouth, but the title was already taken. Otherwise we may all have now been eating portsmouths! (Thank heavens he never went anywhere near Ramsbottom.)

The sandwich has always been a finger food – whether served as part of tea or eaten at lunchtime. The exception would be 'open' sandwiches, which are eaten with cutlery.

Bluffers should know that tea sandwiches must have their crusts cut off, and presented either in the shape of triangles, rectangles or – as the Royal Household prefer – in small squares. Don't ever serve them in large diagonal cross cuts, because they'll look like something you bought in a garage forecourt (and probably are).

SCONES

Firstly, the pronunciation issue must be addressed. It is always 'skon' never 'skone'. If you use the latter you will be instantly exposed as a fraud, and summarily banned from afternoon tea circles for the rest of your life.

If you have survived that first hurdle, you'll need to move on to history and shape. Scones have suffered somewhat of an identity crisis in the past, and imparting this knowledge tactfully to your fellow guests will impress ever the most seasoned of afternoon tea connoisseurs. Originally scones were triangular, savoury and griddled. Today, they are round, sweet and baked.

Scones are thought to have originated in Scotland, and take their name from the Stone of Scone (although here, the word is pronounced 'skoone', just to confuse the uninitiated).

Traditionally they were not part of the afternoon tea offering and were only really found in the South West of England where the term 'cream tea' originated. The rest of the country continued eating muffins (not those indigestible American things which are now – ironically

– termed an 'English muffin') served with butter and sometimes jam.

Having selected your scone, do not pick up your knife and cut into it. Scones are broken, not cut – just like other bread products at table. A freshly made scone will easily break in two from the middle.

Strawberry jam is traditional, but damson is perhaps the more sophisticated choice, and for those who really profess to know their jams, state a preference for 'bullace' a dusty-coloured member of the plum family. And, of course, clotted cream is the sine qua non. There are many who will spend many fruitful hours arguing as to whether it should be jam then cream or cream then jam. Frankly, there are more pressing things in life … such as ensuring the correct size of napkin (12 inches square, remember). The answer lies in whether you are going Cornish or Devonian. The former like to show off their clotted cream and so place it on top of the jam, whereas Devonians reportedly like their cream seeping into the warm scone below. Both are acceptable, but what is never permissible is to sandwich the two halves together.

If you find yourself being served scones with aerosol cream in a cafe or hotel the only proper thing to do is have the local council close it down immediately.

CAKES & ASSORTED FANCIES

The top layer of the cake stand will be for the cakes. There are no set rules as to what is on offer here – nonetheless, they should be small and dainty and capable of being eaten in a few mouthfuls with the fingers or with a small fork (now usually a pastry fork – which has three tines, note). Cupcakes are not part of a correct afternoon tea.

In tea shops and hotels the tea service favours small French patisseries but in a private house you can expect to see larger cakes, such as a Victoria sponge or fruit cake.

TEA

Food aside, afternoon tea cannot be thus called without the aromatic drink made from the plant *Camellia sinensis*. It originated in China as a medicinal drink, was introduced to Europe by Portuguese traders in the 16th century, and from there to Britain where it became popular in the 17th century. From there it progressively found its way through the British Empire, taking root particularly (and literally) in India and Ceylon where it was deliberately cultivated in order to end China's monopoly on the world tea trade.

Tasting note: tea always tastes better sipped from fine bone china cups and saucers. Anyone who serves you tea in a mug has clearly mistaken you for a tradesman or a chimpanzee.

Class connoisseurs will be carefully watching to see how you are holding your teacup. Hooking your index finger through with your thumb on top of the handle will show you up as a parvenu. The correct way to hold your fine bone china is by making your thumb and index finger meet in the handle. The cup is supported by the handle resting on your middle finger. The little finger does not extend. Ever.

If drinking tea at a low coffee table, the saucer is picked up and held at chest height to catch any drips. If having tea at a higher table then the saucer may remain on it.

How a person stirs their tea is usually a reliable indicator of the class and background of the tea-drinker. Circular motions are reserved for the building site. Back and forth motions (6, 12, 6, 12 – if imagining it as a clock face) are for the cognoscenti. A light flick of the teaspoon above the cup when finished (to shake off the drips) is elegant. Bashing the spoon on the side of the cup is elephant.

BREWING TEMPERATURES FOR TEA

Elementary tea bluffing is to know that not all types of tea are brewed at the same temperature (i.e. you can't just pour boiling water on everything). Usually, the more delicate the tea the lower the temperature used. Using water that is too hot on a green tea, for example, will scald the leaves and produce a very different, bitter taste.

White teas	75°C | 160°F
Green teas	65–80°C | 150–180°F
Oolong teas	88–93°C | 190–200°F
Black teas	90–100°C | 200–212°F
Herbal teas	100°C | 212°F

You can now buy smart kettles where the desired temperature can be set in advance – which will save hosts worrying too much about getting the exact temperature.

Note that herbal teas are not actually teas – they are infusions of plants, herbs and spices. Obviously, all teas served to guests should be loose-leaf. Teabags can only be used when no guests are present and the curtains have been drawn.

WARMING THE POT

Warming the teapot *must* be done before adding the tea leaves. This is absolutely essential.

1. Boil the kettle, wait a few moments and pour in just under a third of the hot water.
2. Swish the water around the pot. This helps the next batch of water stay warm so the tea leaves open and release their best flavour. Once warmed, the water can be tipped away ready for the freshly boiled batch.
3. Add in the required amount of tea. The old adage 'one per person and one for the pot' is generally nonsense as this can result in a very strong tea. Two teaspoons for three people is generally a good guide.
4. Leave to steep/brew for three to six minutes – depending on size of leaf and how strong you like your tea (larger leaves need longer).

TEA DANCES

Known as *'thé dansant'* in French, the tea dance is a natural progression from afternoon tea and can actually incorporate it. This, too, is experiencing a resurgence of interest – not least because it is much less expensive than a formal dinner or ball (no bluffer will ever admit that expense is a consideration) and it ticks many of the same boxes and has a certain novelty value – even though it reached the zenith of its popularity in the late 19th century in suburban Britain. In fact, you might add knowledgeably to anybody interested in the fathomless depths of your expertise in these matters, that tea dances were made fashionable by Victorian Royal Navy officers who figured out that they were an effective means of inveigling young women to come aboard ship in the late afternoon, when a more formal affair in the evening would have required chaperones and stricter observance of etiquette.

Typical refreshments were tea, lemonade, chocolates, sandwiches, biscuits and cakes. Increasingly, wine and Champagne made an appearance (it hadn't escaped the dashing naval officers' attention that it had the effect of lowering the young ladies' inhibitions).

Bluffers on a budget might think about using the 'function room' of a pub or club, where the natural inclination of revellers will be to repair to the bar to continue the party when the dance is over. The advantage of this is that there is no expectation that you, as host, should foot the bar bill (although you might generally offer to buy a first drink to encourage your guests to stay on).

Music should ideally be provided by a string quintet (able to play the charleston).

BED & BREAKFAST

From time to time you will find yourself obliged to offer a guest, or guests, a bed for the night – especially if they have travelled some distance to attend your soirée. This is to be avoided if possible, because it means that your work will not finish until they have left the following day (hopefully) and some of them will expect to stay for lunch. If so, invite them for breakfast or brunch instead because that way they'll be less inclined to remain much after 12.30pm. The end time is implicit.

But if you have no choice (and some of us willingly make the choice) there are certain rules about how to host your guests overnight.

GUEST ROOMS

First things first, a clean guest room is not a luxury: it is a must if you want to be taken seriously as a host. Guests should expect to be able to sleep in comfort and cleanliness. Dirt and untidiness may not faze you but it may be beyond the pale for most people even if they say nothing. On the other hand, there can be some advantages to not cleaning properly – your guests will only stay with you again as a last resort.

FOR THE BEDROOM …

Bedding White bedding, for all bedrooms, works best and matches any décor. Make sure that you invest in the finest Egyptian cotton with a decent thread count. Whatever the colour, make sure it's ironed. You can't do luxury with creased linens. Even if you don't iron your own bedding (who does?), iron the guests'.

Storage Make sure the guests have plenty of storage space – keep bedside tables, chests of drawers and wardrobes empty. If you have limited storage space in your home then empty the contents of drawers and cupboards in the guest bedroom into a large box and stow it away in your own bedroom.

Tissues Check the tissue box is not about to run out before the guests' arrival.

Water Always leave a carafe of water and some glasses, or failing the carafe – some bottles (although bottles of branded mineral water can make it look more like a hotel than a private residence). Fill the carafe just before the guest is due to arrive or else the vessel will have water bubbles, or subaquatic organisms, which show just how long the water has been sitting there.

Wardrobe Ensure that there is plenty of space to hang clothes in the wardrobe and offer a range of hangers: padded hangers for ladies' dresses, standard hangers (wood preferably, plastic if you must – but definitely no wire ones) and a jacket hanger.

FOR THE BATHROOM …

Door hook Somewhere to hang their dressing gowns, or clothes when showering. This is often overlooked.

Dressing gown This is what the Americans call a 'robe'. It is emphatically not a robe, it is a dressing gown. Never make this mistake, even to an American. Correct them politely but firmly point out that when in Rome, do as the British do. English is our language, and former colonists are permitted to use it with our permission – but occasionally they must strive harder to get it right.

Shampoo and body wash Both should be left in the shower, or in or near the bath. And don't forget to clean watermarks and remove matted hair and toenails from plugs.

Lavatory paper A full, new lavatory roll should await your guests, with several spare rolls within reach.

Spare toiletries Some disorganised guests arrive having forgotten some toiletries, or – worse – not having packed any at all. Don't have spare toothbrushes, toothpaste, moisturisers, deodorants and the like on display – but keep them in the bathroom cabinet, which most guests will look in anyway. It's usually a good idea to leave a stock of painkillers in there as well.

Shelves and cupboards Ensure you have a clear shelf or cabinet for the contents of your guests' washbags.

Towels As with bedding, white is often a smart colour of choice. For each person leave a bath and hand towel, and don't forget the bath and shower mats. And setting out a flannel that's a darker colour is often appreciated by guests who will use it to help remove their make-up and then won't fret about staining it too much.

BREAKFAST

Breakfast should not be overlooked or ill-considered. It is a vital part of the home entertaining formula.

Although you needn't offer a full, cooked breakfast, having a selection of cereals, breads and bakery items, and perhaps some fresh eggs is a must. It really isn't necessary to provide a buffet of kedgeree and devilled kidneys under silver lids, but it's unlikely that anyone will complain if you do.

Some must-have items in your cupboards for guests' breakfast:

- **Tea and coffee** – English breakfast tea is a safe bet if you don't have room for Earl Grey, an Assam, or Darjeeling. Always make available fresh coffee in at least two different strengths (in a cafetière). Don't even think of suggesting instant.
- **Fruit juice** – fresh orange juice and grapefruit juice.
- **Milk** – for tea and coffee, but also for cereal. Serve in a big jug for breakfast. Ensure that it's semi-skimmed.
- **Cereals** – depending on what else is on offer a choice of a few is a must. Upmarket hosts will make sure they have an exclusive European high-fibre breakfast cereal, often with an impressive-looking crest on the packet. Something like Duchy Originals organic mixed flake with apple should be chosen over Sugar Frosties. (If there are children staying check with their parents before you offer them any sugar-coated cereals.)
- **Eggs** – if you don't know how to poach, fry and

scramble eggs then you have failed as a host. Learn before the next batch of guests presents themselves at your breakfast table – it's not hard, and the personal touch is appreciated.

- **Bread** – choice of white or wholemeal. Or seeded. Or if you really want to prove your breakfast credentials, offer Poilane Sourdough (which freezes superbly).
- **Jams** – have one or two jams, honey and a marmalade (preferably thick cut). Set one teaspoon per pot.
- **Table sauces and ketchups** – not really that compulsory but some guests like these if you are serving hot food. Don't bother about decanting into cut-glass bowls – just ensure that the bottles are clean.
- **Sugar** – don't offer refined white sugar; your guests might think you're trying to kill them. To be honest, brown sugar isn't much better. Offer honey as an alternative, and sweeteners for tea and coffee.
- **Butter** – a neat, fresh stick in a butter dish should be presented, rather than four-day-old butter with crumbs and jammy smear marks all over it.
- **Fruit** – a bowl of fresh fruit will spruce up the table even if not touched.
- **Yoghurt** – some guests, especially from the New World, are particularly fond of something called a probiotic.

Finally, if your guests ask you what time you'd like them to be down for breakfast the correct answer is 'Whenever you like.' Try not to arrive after the guests; it'll give them far too much opportunity to go through your cupboards and fridge to see how you *really* eat.

PROGRAMME OF ACTIVITIES

If your guests are staying for more than a few days, especially over holiday periods such as Christmas or Easter, then it is prudent for hosts to have a range of outings and activities arranged. You needn't produce a schedule and running order, but giving them options is always a good idea. Suggest a walk to the pub for a lunchtime drink, but always make sure that you have a good selection of waterproofs available (even if it's sunny when you set out). And if the pub is further than a mile or so, do a car drop in advance or arrange to get a taxi back. For some reason the return walk is always far less interesting than the outbound.

DUTIES OF A HOUSE GUEST

Allergies Upon accepting the invitation to stay, your guests should alert you to any allergies or intolerances they may have. These can range from being deathly allergic to feather pillows or domestic pets, to being gluten (or children) intolerant.

Tip for hosts: If you have the space and budget, keeping some hypoallergenic or fully allergy-proof bedding for sensitive guests is always a good idea. Washing bedding with non-biological washing detergent is also good practice as biological detergents can make people's skin break out in rashes. So can bed bugs, those unwanted house guests which require special pest control measures to eradicate. Unfortunately they're almost impossible to detect until the infestation is well established. If that happens you'll soon know about it.

Hostess gift As has been discussed earlier in this guide, a guest should never turn up empty handed if they are staying with you. If they are staying for longer than one night then their gift should reflect this. Don't expect the presentation to be made on arrival or during the stay. It is perfectly acceptable for your guests to make a parting gift. But ideally they should make two, one when they arrive and another when they depart.

Help! No one is ever too grand to offer help to the hosts, and you should never be too grand to refuse it. If the guests are staying for more than four days, you might reasonably expect them to offer to cook (and buy the ingredients) or, better still, invite you out to a local restaurant.

Damage If they break it, they pay for it. Although most hosts will graciously decline any offer to remunerate them for loss or damage, the gesture will be noted and appreciated.

Offering to strip the bed Thoughtful guests will ask whether they should strip the bed before leaving. Good hosts will never dream of asking guests to do this, but again will appreciate the offer.

Tipping staff If you are staying in a house with staff, especially staff that have been looking after you and your guests, then it is usually the done thing to leave a tip for them when you leave. Ensure that the proferred gift is witnessed by more than one staff member if it is meant to be shared.

'In a restaurant choose a table near a waiter.'

(Jewish proverb)

EATING OUT

The Chinese do not entertain in their own houses (or indeed anyone else's). Instead they will invite close friends, family and business clients to a restaurant. This is not necessarily because they are ashamed of their homes but because they feel a restaurant is more likely to put people at ease than their private living space. But entertaining in a restaurant is not strictly an Asian cultural choice and sometimes it can make sense for those of us in the Western world to entertain our guests in a public setting instead of a more domestic one. Especially if we live in modest circumstances and don't have a separate wing for the servants.

There is still an expected form to observe. Your choice of restaurant is, naturally, key to your success. You don't really want to take friends who might be having money troubles to a Michelin-starred restaurant (even if you are going to pay) as this will just make them feel more miserable about their circumstances. Similarly, if you love Southeast Asian cuisine but know your guests are less gastronomically adventurous then (even though you are going to pay) opt for somewhere with a more parochial menu.

GREETING GUESTS

If you are meeting friends or family and you have booked a table then make sure you are first to arrive, and wait at the table. If you are entertaining a client or a senior colleague then it is the done thing to wait for them at the front of the restaurant, having arrived and made sure your table is suitable. If it isn't, then ask to be moved, and if that's denied then adopt your most incredulous look (as if to say 'You clearly have no idea who I am have you?') – you'd be amazed how quickly *maître d*'s can change their minds if they think you might leave. Of course, it's a classic bluff, and you'll just have to hope that it isn't called. Standing outside a restaurant and telling your guests there has been a change of plan is not a good start to lunch or dinner.

CLOAKROOM ETIQUETTE

Gone are the days when there was always a separate little cloakroom, or vestibule, just before you entered the main dining room for you to shed your coats, scarves and bags. Today you are frequently expected to divest in the same room as the diners, so it's never a good idea to turn up over-dressed. If your guests do happen to be encumbered by coats, ensure that a member of staff is hovering to collect them. This can be easily ensured by tipping in advance when they collect yours. A five-pound note usually does the trick; ten pounds means that they will keep a close and attentive eye on your table throughout the meal.

TECHNOLOGY AT THE TABLE

Mobiles and other technology should really be switched off (or to silent) when arriving at the table. Some enterprising diners might play a game with friends and colleagues where everyone puts their telephone on the table, on vibrate, and the first to touch their phone pays for the entire meal.

A good bluffing ruse is to arrange for a colleague to text you shortly after your guests have arrived, giving the impression that you're busy and in demand. Don't answer, but apologise effusively and switch your phone off immediately in full sight and hearing of everyone. This shows that you will suffer no further distractions and that your guests will have your full attention.

NEVER answer a telephone call while at the table. It's very bad form.

ORDERING

It is far smarter to order without looking at the menu. It suggests a certain familiarity with the restaurant and is another good reason for arriving before your guests. Decide what you are having in advance, and remember your choices when the waiter comes to the table. You really only have to remember two courses (pudding is ordered later).

When your guests arrive, it's a good idea to ask if they'd like a glass of 'fizz'. They might think they're getting Champagne, but you will previously have ordered a glass of ordinary 'Crémant Brut' or similar sparkling wine, which is frequently indistinguishable to anybody but an expert. You will point it out to your waiter saying '[insert number here] More of the same please.' These will be brought to the table ready-poured at about a quarter of the cost of a run-of-the-mill Champagne.

Ask for the wine list to be given to you as host. You will, of course, have perused it in advance and established what the house wine is. Order a bottle (or, depending on numbers, bottles) of red and white house wine by the *label*. If your waiter or sommelier should have the temerity to say 'Would that be the house wine Sir/Madam?', hold your nerve and say 'What an excellent choice of *vin de maison*! Congratulations on the quality of your cellar.' And then, with a wry aside to your guests say: 'You should always judge a restaurant's cellar by their choice of house wine. It's a well-known rule of thumb. Rest assured that this is excellent.'

Don't forget to ensure that the waiter asks each guest when he/she takes their order if they would like to drink something other than wine. For some curious reason, some people prefer water.

If ordering a bottle, remember not to actually taste the wine or perform elaborate gestures and swirls. All you need do is simply sniff the wine to see if it is corked (an unmistakeable smell not unlike a wet dog freshly rolled in rotting compost). The taste is irrelevant. Even if it's not quite to your taste, if it's not corked, you're still paying for it.

PAYING THE BILL

Britons seem to suffer no end of awkwardness and embarrassment when it comes to paying the bill. There need never be any confusion again if simple rules are followed. The person who does the inviting pays. Depending on how things go the invitees return the compliment at some future date (again, within six months). Of course, there will be occasions when you're eating out with friends and no single individual is the host. In these circumstances different rules apply, and the bill will usually be shared. What must be avoided at all costs is each diner totting up their own bills, itemising who had what. This is where many begin to lose the will to live. Nothing ruins a nice evening more than maths. Everyone should order something of a similar value, and if someone did order something that was a bit more expensive then that person should offer to leave the tip. The only exception to the dread question of itemisation is to excuse non-drinkers in a restaurant party from contributing to the drinks bill. In Britain this invariably exceeds the food bill by a factor of 2 to 1 and can prove ruinously expensive.

Finally, on a first date don't go 'Dutch'. They don't even go Dutch in Holland.

GRATUITOUS GRATUITY

Restaurants in the UK have recently decided that 12.5% is the magic number when it comes to a 'gratuity'. It used to be 10%, for that was very easy for everyone to work out and a nice solid number. Now, it's 12.5%, pretty much close enough to 10% ... close enough for restaurants to get away with it, anyway. Remember – whatever percentage is added this is optional and if the service has been rubbish, it is within your right as a customer to ask for it to be deducted from the bill ... but be prepared to justify this to the head waiter.

There's no point in pretending that you know everything about entertaining – nobody does (including those who write about it for a living). But if you've got this far and absorbed at least a modicum of the information and advice contained within these pages, then you will almost certainly know more than 99% of the rest of the human race about what it takes to be a good host, the rules you must follow, the mistakes you must avoid, and how to pretend to know more about entertaining than you do. What you now do with this information is up to you, but here's a suggestion: be confident about your new-found knowledge, see how far it takes you, but above all, have fun using it. You are now a fully fledged expert in one of humankind's most valued and unique traditions – the gift of cordiality and hospitality to guests and strangers.

And if you remember just one piece of advice, frequently repeated throughout these pages, it is this: make all your guests feel welcome, don't forget their names, and don't run out of food or drink.

GLOSSARY

A list Something all guests should aspire to be featured on.

Bishop of Norwich If his name is mentioned, it usually means that someone is hogging the Port. It might be you.

Brown Sugar A well-known Rolling Stones song often played at functions with a multi-generational guest list so that the DJ can amuse himself by encouraging every man over 50 to attempt a Mick Jagger impression. Sadly, they don't need much persuading. (*See* 'Embarrassing Dad Syndrome').

Bouncer A regrettable necessity at many functions and parties, this is the hired muscle on the door who keeps out the riff-raff. Unfortunately, they usually turn out to be worse than the riff-raff. Best advice is to hire a retired Gurkha – polite, charming, professional and utterly effective with the strong-arm stuff when necessary.

Carriages A euphemism for the preferred time to go after a party. Slightly pretentious, but nevertheless a polite way of saying 'clear off'.

Close-up magician Also known as a mentalist or micro-magician, these are entertainers who specialise in sleight of hand or mind reading in small groups. Can be hugely enjoyable unless you're mid-flow with an amusing anecdote when they start performing next to you.

Cracker A festive explosive device containing a novelty gift of limited value or interest; also how Uncle Len describes every female under 70.

Embarrassing Dad Syndrome A strange affliction affecting fathers of brides and children celebrating significant birthdays. When they finally realise what the festivities are costing them, a glazed and desperate look is generally followed by an ill-advised attempt to prove that they can still 'throw some moves' on the dance floor. Invariably accompanied by brides and/or vulnerable children holding their heads and repeating 'Please, God, no, make it stop.' (*See* 'Brown Sugar'.)

Helium A gas used to fill balloons; also to fill buffoons who think squeaky voices are hugely amusing.

Hollywood entrance Derogatory term for a method of arrival by hosts who keep their guests waiting and then arrive in an over-the-top fashion by helicopter, Harley Davidson or parachute. Good hosts are already firmly in place to welcome their guests.

Maraschino cherries 'Glass fruit' used in cocktails for decoration. Some drinkers even eat them. They wouldn't if they knew how they are made. Pitted cherries are bleached in a solution of calcium chloride and sulphur dioxide and then given a bath in artificial colouring and flavouring. Delicious if you like chemicals.

Mixer A person considered in terms of their ability (or not) to interact socially with others. Also something added to a spirit to disguise the taste.

PBO Initialism for 'Pending Better Offer'. A potential guest who earns a reputation for delaying acceptance to a party or event to see if something better comes along in the meantime.

Punch A dangerous and toxic brew, best avoided on the grounds that nobody has any idea what's in it – including the host, who's probably using it as an excuse to get rid of some half-used bottles of disgusting sticky liqueur and old hair gel.

Sardines A well-known, traditional 'parlour' game, which is essentially an adult version of 'Hide-and-seek'. Apparently much favoured by Queen Victoria, possibly because her voluminous skirts were an obvious place for guests to hide (with room to spare for much of the Commonwealth).

Secret Santa Guests at a dinner party are randomly assigned a person in advance to whom they anonymously give a Christmas present up to an agreed (usually low) budget. The general idea is that they find a novelty gift which reflects the giftee's personality and interests. A 99p remaindered copy of Tony Blair's *A Journey* would be the obvious choice for someone of unashamedly jingoistic views.

Shaken, not shhtirred An expression which should never be repeated to a professional bartender when requesting a cocktail. Everyone has their breaking point.

Shot girl Usually the impressively pneumatic teenaged daughter of a guest who wouldn't otherwise be invited.

She is identified by a low-slung 'shot belt' containing shot glasses and two bottles of hard spirits (usually both of them tequila, a spirit made from the indigestible agave plant, better ingested in a single gulp without pausing to savour).

Six or ten The right numbers for a dinner party. Eight rarely works, because there'll always be one person speaking and seven listening. With ten guests, conversation usually divides evenly; with six, everybody gets an opportunity to join in.

Table rotation In principle a good idea, whereby dinner guests are invited to move after each course, or just the main course. Usually works best at business functions where the host and co-hosts stay put and the guests revolve around them. Less effective in a social context where people are having an interesting conversation and are less inclined to move.

Vodka luge A curious and not always tasteful ice sculpture, which involves the swift and unimpeded passage of a generous measure of chilled vodka into the mouth of a recumbent and foolishly receptive drinker. For some reason, the recipient is deluded into thinking that this method is less intoxicating than drinking vodka neat from a bottle. It isn't.

Z list A list of party guests you really don't want to see your name on.

A BIT MORE BLUFFING...

Available from all good bookshops

bluffers.com